LIGHT VERSE ON HEAVY TOPICS

Also by Erika S. Fine

How It Happened: The 2016 Presidential Campaign in Jest and Verse

LIGHT VERSE
ON HEAVY TOPICS

*Pandemic, Politics,
and Pandemonium*

Erika S. Fine

POET PUNDIT PRESS

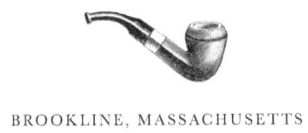

BROOKLINE, MASSACHUSETTS

Poet Pundit Press

Paperback: 979-8-218-18139-0
Cover and Book design by Mayfly Design

Library of Congress Catalog Number: 2023906184

To my mother, Elsa Honig Fine

*Without her, I would still be working on
this book, perhaps procrastinating forever.*

CONTENTS

Introduction

When you can't get out of bed,
Write a poem instead.

When the news induces dread,
Write a poem instead.

When absurdity has spread,
Write a poem instead.

Don't despair or cry or flee—
Set your mind to poetry.

That is how this book of rhymes
Sprouted in these stressful times.

The inspiration for this poem was a *New York Times* op-ed by Sarah Ruhl, a playwright and essayist, from the outset of the pandemic (March 13, 2020): "Broadway Is Closed. Write Poems Instead."

The poems in this book cover 2018 through 2022, with a few earlier ones in the final chapter.

A handful of the poems in this book—in most cases, a slightly different version of them—were published in the *New York Times*, *Light* (a journal of light verse), and Cognoscenti (the website for WBUR, an NPR station in Boston).

2018

2018 was an unnerving year. Special Counsel Robert Mueller continued the investigation he began in May 2017 into Russian interference in the 2016 U.S. election. Trump's affair with an adult-film actress came to light, as did hush money his personal lawyer paid her. Mass shootings horrified and scarred the country, including massacres at a high school in Parkland, Florida, and a synagogue in Pittsburgh, Pennsylvania. Thousands of children were separated from their parents as a result of the Trump administration's immigration policy. Trump held a summit meeting with Russian dictator Vladimir Putin in Helsinki, seeming to favor him over America's allies. Multiple wildfires devastated California. Trump nominated Brett Kavanaugh, a right-wing federal judge, to the U.S. Supreme Court. Kavanaugh's confirmation hearing—televised before a riveted nation—was contentious, centering on an allegation of sexual assault when he was in high school. The chief takeaway for many viewers (or perhaps the only thing everyone agreed on) was that Kavanaugh likes beer. On a cheerier note, Prince Harry of Great Britain married a woman he probably couldn't have wed a generation ago—a divorced, bi-racial American actress.

Hostility to Stability
January 8, 2018

If the "genius is stable"
Then why is Trump unable
To distinguish truth from fiction?
(And to use coherent diction?)

If Trump's the "smartest ever"
Then why can't he endeavor
To learn the role our Fourth Estate
Must play to keep our nation *great*?

When Michael Wolff and Henry Holt
Produced a book-length thunderbolt,
Trump wished that he could re-address
The libel laws that guide our press.

"Oh where, oh where is my Roy Cohn?"
He wondered with a loathsome moan.
From Roy he learned to have no scruples—
Yes, Trump was one of Cohn's best pupils.

~~~~~~~~~~~~~~~~~~~~~~~~~~~~~~~~~~~~~

Donald Trump, a self-described "stable genius," did not seem to understand that a free press—the Fourth Estate—is one of the foundations of our country. He has long shown hostility to the press, routinely dismissing unflattering—but true—reporting as "fake news." Press freedom, of course, includes the right to criticize government officials. In January 2018, Henry Holt & Company published a book by journalist Michael Wolff, *Fire and Fury: Inside the Trump White House*, that depicts an incompetent and dysfunctional Trump administration. Trump tried to block the book's publication and threatened to "take a strong look at" U.S. libel laws to make it easier to sue writers and publishers. The same week that Wolff's book was released, the press reported that Trump had asked "Where's my Roy Cohn?" when then-Attorney General Jeff Sessions, against Trump's wishes,

recused himself from the Justice Department's investigation into Russian inter-
ference in the 2016 presidential election. (The disreputable, take-no-prisoners
lawyer Roy Cohn, known for his role in the McCarthy hearings in the 1950s, was
a mentor and defender of the young Trump.) Trump's remark indicated that
he thought the U.S. attorney general's role was to protect the president, rather
than to serve the American people.

Bold and Golden

January 9, 2018

Oprah's big speech at the glam Golden Globes
Lit up the neurons in Dems' frontal lobes.
Meryl was beaming and Seth Meyers gushing,
But—let's be real—perhaps we are rushing.
It's true that the speech was impassioned and stirring,
But I am not certain that I am concurring
That running for POTUS is what she should do—
She'll *first* need to study a topic or two,
Like governing, politics, treaties, and trade,
Then add immigration, and how laws are made,
And NATO and healthcare and oil and drilling.
That's quite a big "ask," but she just might be willing,
And *then* we may see a campaign that is thrilling—
Two billionaires vying to win the top billing!
She'd kindle excitement and get out the vote
She might be the best anti-Trump antidote.
For every last sexist and bigoted tweet,
She'd prove he was wrong, with an overdue feat:
A brilliant Black female as head of a land
Where votes of Black women were doubly banned.
Black women, they saved us from dreadful Roy Moore,
And nationwide, *they* have more *power* in store.
It is likely that Oprah would soar in the polls
With her noble beliefs and her broadminded goals.
Yes, pop-idol politics may be the rage
In this internet-driven, Kardashian age,
So perhaps we should choose a celebrity who
Can reverse Donald's damage and lead us anew!

At the 2018 Golden Globes, hosted by Seth Meyers on January 7, Oprah Winfrey delivered an inspiring speech about injustice and inequality, with a promise for change. Her speech ignited calls for her to run for president in 2020, against Donald Trump. (Another suggestion: "Perhaps she is better off running as veep / If TV to POTUS is too big a leap.") Two months before the Golden Globes, Roy Moore, a far-right Republican, ran for a U.S. Senate seat in Alabama. His opponent was Doug Jones, a Democrat who, as the chief federal prosecutor in Northern Alabama from 1997 to 2001, helped put two Klu Klux Klan members behind bars for the heinous Birmingham church bombing that killed four African American girls in 1963. During the campaign, several women accused Roy Moore of sexual misconduct or impropriety; some were minors at the time of the alleged misconduct. Moore lost the Senate race, in spite of Trump's endorsement. Many political observers credited Black women in Alabama for driving Moore's defeat in a traditionally Republican state.

The State of the Unions

January 30, 2018

The state of the union of Trump and his wife
Is "Stormy" and hellish and loaded with strife.
The state of the union of Donald and Mitch
Is glee over tax cuts that pamper the rich.
The state of the union of Trump and McCain
Is rarely accordance and mostly disdain.
The state of the union of Trump and his base
Is solid, but sadly, our nation's disgrace.

~~~~~~~~~~~~~~~

Written immediately after Trump's State of the Union address on January 30, 2018, this poem contemplates the fate and state of other Trump "unions"—his partnerships with Senate Majority Leader Mitch McConnell (R-KY), Senator John McCain (R-AZ), and First Lady Melania Trump (the latter in light of news reports on Trump's alleged affair with an adult-film actress with the stage name Stormy Daniels).

Little Donald's Big Parade

February 11, 2018

A draft-dodging rich kid, a no-show in 'Nam,
He faked faulty feet for a doctor's exam.
He yearns for a showy and pompous parade,
A desperate, despot-like power charade,
A gaudy exhibit of strength and of might
To flatter a fraud who was too scared to fight,
With Army tanks, fighter jets serving as props
To prove to the world that Donald is tops!

~~~~~~~~~~~~~~~~~~~~~~~~~~~~

Early in 2018, Trump ordered the Pentagon to plan a military parade in Washington, D.C., with marching soldiers, weaponry, and rolling tanks. He was roundly criticized by both Democrats and Republicans, with one retired general stating, "Donald Trump has continually shown himself to have authoritarian tendencies, and this is just another worrisome example." Although the U.S. holds military parades to mark the end of a war and celebrate returning troops, peacetime shows of power run counter to America's traditions. "We have avoided doing this kind of display, in part to emphasize [the] contrast [with] authoritarian countries," said Julian Zelizer, a historian at Princeton University. Senator Lindsey Graham (R-SC) expressed a similar view, stating that although he "didn't mind a parade honoring the service and sacrifice of our military members," he did not want "a Soviet-style hardware display—that's not who we are. It's kind of cheesy. I think it shows weakness." Likewise, Adam Gopnik in the *New Yorker* wrote that a parade, for Trump, "seems to compensate for insecurity by bloat, show, and trophy" (February 7, 2018). (Trump ultimately called off the parade.)

Another Day at the Office

February 15, 2018

If Obama's attorney had secretly sent
A check to a porn star to try to prevent
A leak to reporters regarding a tryst,
Would Obama receive just a slap on the wrist?
No, Fox would condemn him—self-righteously, snidely—
And Breitbart would cover it, brashly and widely.
The G.O.P. brass would say ethical slips—
Like flings with young women who might have loose lips—
Put our country at risk; damn Obama's not cautious!
Yet for Trump, it's a typical day at the office.

News of Donald Trump's $130,00 payment to silence a porn star did not outrage Republican leaders and right-wing media, even though minor "transgressions" by President Obama infuriated them. The classic example: their outrage when Obama wore a tan summer suit at an August press conference, with some even calling it an "impeachable offense" or security risk.

An Olympic Distraction

February 20, 2018

I heard that he broke his own record for tweeting.
I'd rather watch skiers break records competing.
I'm *glad* Mueller's probe is at long last unfurling.
I'll focus when Finland is finished with curling.
If there was collusion, will Trump pay a price?
Not sure, but those Russians are magic on ice.
His tweets were bizarre on the Russian indictment.
I much prefer short-track for gripping excitement.
I think he is Vladimir's gullible stooge.
Perhaps, but I think it's now time for the luge.
With Trump, our great country is being diminished.
I'll ponder it once the Olympics are finished. . . .

~~~~~~~~~~~~~~~~~~

In February 2018, coverage of the Winter Olympics competed with news about Trump's political and sexual affairs. Many viewers welcomed the distraction of the Olympics, especially after Trump's belligerent, hours-long tweetstorm on a variety of grievances (February 17–18). He was particularly angry that Special Counsel Robert Mueller had indicted, on February 16, thirteen Russians for interfering in the 2016 election to help Trump and disparage Hillary Clinton. The indictment stated that the Russians "communicated with unwitting individuals associated with the Trump campaign," but it did not address whether anyone on Trump's team had knowingly colluded with the Russians.

A Modest Proposal

February 24, 2018

"To prevent further shootings in schools, we'll arm teachers,
And for safety in churches, let's also arm preachers.
For protection in gyms, we'll give guns to the trainers,
And for theater and musicals? Armed entertainers!
Then for City Hall safety, we'll arm all the mayors.
And for ballparks in peril, we'll arm all the players.
For a nightclub at risk, we'll give guns to the deejays,
And for driving to all, let's sell guns on the freeways.

We know Donald will guide us; he'll get his own gun,
An immense one that's potent and second to none.
With his tiny hands itching to finger the trigger,
He'll be scary and huge, with an ego much bigger.
And *then* we'll become a secure and strong nation.
With everyone armed—no more fear or frustration!
In one hand a phone, in the other a gun—
And day-to-day life will be safe, even fun!"

Parkland Students' Response

"Wait, *arming* the nation is no way to go!
Our stance on your plan is a clear-cut 'hell, NO!'
Look, *this* is our *life*, not a video *game!*
The gun lobby's money is largely to blame.
You G.O.P. lawmakers cower in fear
That your N.R.A. sustenance might disappear.
This *isn't* a fifties film starring John Wayne
(And even he'd know this solution's insane).
This Wild West fantasy view of our nation
Will lead to more killings and loss, not cessation.
To hell with the N.R.A.'s lobbying poison.
Let's make this land safer to raise girls and boys in!"

On February 14, 2018, a 19-year-old gunman entered Marjory Stoneman Douglas High School in Parkland, Florida, and opened fire on students and faculty. He killed seventeen people and wounded seventeen others. It was the deadliest high-school shooting in American history. In response, Trump and other Republicans dodged gun-safety questions and recommended arming teachers in their classrooms. Trump tweeted, "Highly trained, gun adept, teachers/coaches would solve the problem instantly, before police arrive." Many observers criticized or ridiculed the G.O.P.'s proposed solution, noting that a sheriff's deputy, armed and in uniform, failed to enter the school building and confront the shooter, and that three other officers, when they arrived on the scene, remained positioned behind their cars and also failed to confront the shooter. Even so, the predominant Republican position was that the way to deal with the proliferation of guns and killings was to increase the proliferation of guns. (Note: Remarks about Trump's small hands have been around since 1988, when *Spy* magazine called him a "short-fingered vulgarian." Trump hates the "short-fingered" allegation and has disputed it for years.)

They Made America Great Again!

March 25, 2018

They "Marched for Their Lives" and their speeches brought cheers.
Their insights and eloquence also brought tears.
Although they can't vote yet, they carried their weight,
And thousands of kids made America great!

Could *this* be the start of a nationwide movement
That will, at long last, lead to gun-law improvement?

~~~~~~~~~~~~~~~~~~~~~~~~~~~~~~~~~~~~~~~

After the school shooting in Parkland, Florida, a group of surviving students planned a large march to support gun-safety legislation. The event, known as March for Our Lives, took place in Washington, D.C., on March 24, 2018, with about 450 similar rallies held that same day throughout the country. The speakers—all students, some in high school and others as young as eleven—addressed the crowd in D.C. The rallies drew prominent political figures, including former Arizona Representative Gabby Giffords, herself a survivor of gun violence. Kamala Harris, then a U.S. senator, participated in the Los Angeles rally. Attendance across the U.S. was estimated to be between 1.2 and 2 million, making March for Our Lives one of the biggest protests in American history.

Speaker Madness

April 12, 2018

Two G.O.P. Speakers surprised us this week:
Paul Ryan announced he would no longer seek
A seat in the House—he will give up his spot—
And Boehner announced that he's now selling pot!

~~~~~~

On April 11, 2018, Speaker of the House Paul Ryan (R-WI)—once considered a Republican party "golden boy"—announced his retirement from elective politics. At the time, he was 48 years old, with a vice presidential nomination and two decades as a U.S. congressman under his belt. The same day, the public learned that former Speaker of the House John Boehner (R-OH), once staunchly opposed to legalized marijuana, was joining the board of a large cannabis company. He explained that his thinking on marijuana had "evolved." (The title of the poem is a play on the name of the notorious anti-cannabis film from the 1930s.)

Intervention

April 14, 2018

With Comey's new book getting plenty of press
What's giving dear Donald the greatest distress?
The prostitute pee-party Putin-paid capers
Appearing (again) in our coast-to-coast papers!

Diversions from this is what Donald desired—
By whom was the president duly inspired?

By *President Clinton's* big bombs-as-distraction
From news of impeachment and intern-attraction!
But people cared more about Bill's little lies
Than faraway missiles in faraway skies.

For Donald, the leading diversion criteria
Were "huge" and "explosive," like bombing in Syria!
But bombing, for him, was a big contravention:
The *candidate* Trump favored nonintervention.

With Bolton aboard now and Comey's book brewing,
The only way forward was Donald's pursuing
A bombing attack to stop chemical strikes—
A strategy *Hillary* said that she likes!
Campaigning, he claimed she's too *quick* to use force,
Did ego or impulse make Donald change course?

In April 2018, former F.B.I. Director James Comey's book, *A Higher Loyalty: Truth, Lies, and Leadership*, generated headlines across the country, even before its release. The book called Trump's presidency a "forest fire" and described the president as "unethical" and "untethered to truth." Perhaps more embarrassing for Trump was the book's claim that he was fixated on refuting the allegation that the Russian government had taped him watching prostitutes urinate on a

Moscow hotel bed. While promoting the book in a television interview, Comey said he thought it was "possible" that the prostitute incident had actually occurred. The president, of course, was livid about the book's portrayal of him. On April 13, Trump, encouraged by John Bolton, the new national security advisor (as of April 9), ordered the U.S. military to bomb Syria in retaliation for a suspected chemical-weapons attack. This reminded many of August 1998, when President Bill Clinton announced unexpected U.S. missile attacks on terrorist-related targets in Afghanistan and Sudan. At that time, many people, even those who supported the missile strikes, wondered whether the president was hoping to shift attention away from the Monica Lewinsky matter. Did Trump employ a similar bombs-as-distraction strategy? During the presidential campaign, he had criticized Hillary Clinton's hawkish, interventionist views.

Put That Phone Away!

April 23, 2018

I went out to dinner, relaxed, and sat back,
But glanced at my phone and saw "Bombing attack!"

I plopped on my couch—I was weary and tired—
But glanced at my phone and saw "Tillerson fired!"

I went for a walk—it was balmy and sunny—
But glanced at my phone and saw "Stormy got money!"

I went to a bar to hang out and unwind,
But glanced at my phone and saw "Ryan resigned!"

My team was ahead and I got so excited,
But glanced at my phone and saw "Russians indicted!"

I practiced my tennis, a sport I am slow in,
But glanced at my phone and saw "Big raid on Cohen!"

I ordered my latté with milk extra foamy,
But glanced at my phone and saw "New book by Comey!"

While reading Walt Whitman (though poems often bore me),
I glanced at my phone and saw more news on Stormy.

I tossed out my smartphone and bought an old fliptop.
My anguish is down and my outlook is tiptop!

In the first third of 2018, major news stories and compelling headlines were non-stop. Trump bombed Syria without congressional authorization, and he fired Secretary of State Rex Tillerson. Trump's affair with adult-film actress Stormy Daniels—and the hush money to cover it up—provided endless clickbait. U.S. Congressman Paul Ryan (R-WI), Speaker of the House and the 2012 Republican vice presidential candidate, decided not to run for re-election. Special Counsel Robert Mueller indicted thirteen Russians for interfering in the 2016 presidential election to benefit Trump. F.B.I. agents raided former Trump lawyer Michael Cohen's office. James Comey's book, *A Higher Loyalty*, portrayed Trump as an unethical, ego-driven liar. And more. It was hard for a news junkie to relax.

Don't Decry Wolf

May 1, 2018

"Ruthless, rude, revolting!"
"Indiscreet, insulting!"

Yes, these were Wolf's severe reviews
From Fox and other right-wing news.

I found this all amusing,
Confounding and confusing—
Just whom are they accusing
Of shamelessly refusing
To act with grace, civility,
Decorum, and humility?

Let's face the facts and come to grips:
Comedians make cracks and quips,
Often barbs that jar us,
Jokes that can provoke us,
Stings and taunts that touch a nerve,
Offered up without reserve.

She did her job with dash and verve.
Her subjects got what they deserve.
Don't chastise *her* for snark and sass—
It's *Trump* who's made our discourse crass.

～～～～～～～～～～～～～

Comedian Michelle Wolf's performance at the White House Correspondents' Association Dinner was provocative, confrontational, and bawdy. Fox News and other allies of the Trump administration denounced her performance, but so did mainstream journalists and even the president of the association. Should they have? The correspondents' association knowingly hired a nervy, edgy comedian, and when she spoke up about the ills of the Trump administration, the association should have backed her. As a friend phrased it, "She spoke truth to power after a year of power speaking lies to the press." (The thin-skinned and crass Trump did not attend the dinner, even though presidents normally do.)

Assorted Sordid Stories

May 5, 2018

The porn star was paid right before the election
So Trump's indiscretion could sidestep detection.

————

The election and payoff had *zero* connection—
The payment was made for his family's protection.

————

The tryst never happened and Stormy is lying—
Her silence alone is what Trump's team was buying.

————

The hush money wasn't at Donald's behest—
He trusted Mike Cohen to do what was best.

So Cohen paid Stormy and Trump did not know,
But Rudy said Donald refunded the dough.

————

Though truth can be stranger than fiction, it's wise
To sync up your stories and *then* offer lies.

The Stormy-Trump saga is sordid and mangled.
Perhaps it will never be fully untangled.

~~~~~~~~~~~~~~~~~~~~~~~~~~~~~~~~

In October 2016, shortly before the 2016 presidential election, Michael Cohen, Trump's personal lawyer at the time, paid Stormy Daniels, an adult-film actress, $130,000 to keep her quiet about an alleged sexual encounter with Trump a decade earlier. The *Wall Street Journal* revealed the alleged affair and payoff in January 2018. In early May 2018, the explanation of the payment to Daniels kept changing. Rudy Giuliani, Trump's new personal attorney, first suggested that the payment was made to keep Daniels quiet in the run-up to the election, a scenario that would likely be a violation of campaign-finance law. Later, Giuliani "clarified" his remark, claiming that the payment was not a campaign-finance violation, since it "was made to resolve a personal and false allegation in order to protect the president's family," and it "would have been done . . . whether he was a candidate or not." There was also confusion about who knew what when. Did Trump authorize the payment, or did Cohen make it on his own? Trump refunded the money to Cohen, but did the president know its purpose? It was hard to sort out the contradictory and shifting accounts.

Self-Destruction

May 8, 2018

We knew that the problem was wider than
Just Spitzer and Weiner—but Schneiderman?

A political rise,
And then a surprise.
I'll try to surmise
What's *wrong* with these guys. . . .

Though power brings laurels,
It sometimes dims morals,
Inflates self-regard,
And leaves others scarred.

~~~~~~~~~~~~~~~~~~~~~~~~~~~~~~~~~~~~~~~

New York Attorney General Eric Schneiderman was a rising star in the Democratic party until four women accused him of physical abuse. Ironically, Schneiderman had been a champion of women's rights and a supporter of the #MeToo movement against sexual harassment. He joined Eliot Spitzer (a fellow Harvard Law School graduate) and Anthony Weiner as liberal New York politicians ruined and disgraced after serious transgressions involving women.

ReMARKLEable!

Prince Harry, still missing his mother, was smitten
With Meghan, a woman who's not from Great Britain.
An American actress descended from slaves,
She might be the luminous icon who saves
The royals from growing outdated and staid—
She's feminist, modern, astute, unafraid.

Their wedding was aired on American screens.
Her mother looked regal in soft muted greens
(An outfit less bright but as nice as the queen's).
The sermon on love and the grand gospel voices
Reflected the novel-for-royalty choices.
The wedding drew millions and millions of views
And finally something trumped Donald in news!

~~~~~~~~~~~~~~~~

On May 19, 2018, American actress Meghan Markle married Prince Harry, the second son of Charles, then Prince of Wales, and the late Diana, Princess of Wales. Although the wedding incorporated some British royal traditions, it departed from them in significant ways. An African American Episcopal bishop delivered a sermon, "The Power of Love," that mentioned Martin Luther King Jr. and alluded to America's history of slavery. A British gospel choir sang "Stand By Me." Meghan's mother looked elegant in a pale green dress-and-coat ensemble, while the queen wore bright lime green (she often wore vivid—almost neon—colors because she knew that people wanted to spot her). The wedding was popular in the United States: approximately 29 million people watched it, surpassing the 23 million who viewed the wedding of Prince William and Kate Middleton.

G7 Summit, Minus One

June 11, 2018

We watched our global standing plummet
When Trump departed from the summit,
And Canada, our longtime friend,
Bemoaned our longtime friendship's end.
But Donald Trump seemed not to care—
He simply wanted Russia there.
And then he left to meet with Kim,
Whose rule is ruthless, harsh, and grim.
Our allies saw Trump's biggest wish
Was being Kim- or Putin-ish—
A despot or an autocrat.
No way would they ally with that.

～～～～～～～～～～～～～～～～

At the annual Group of Seven (G7) summit meeting (the yearly forum of the world's largest countries with advanced economies and representative governments), Trump belligerently confronted America's allies, pushed for Russia's reinstatement into the G7 nations, and quarreled over tariffs and trade. The summit participants, normally cordial and collegial, were stunned and angry at his conduct and demands. Trump left the summit early to meet instead with North Korean dictator Kim Jong-un in Singapore, sending disparaging tweets about Canadian Prime Minister Justin Trudeau on the way there. Most foreign policy experts condemned Trump's behavior. One former diplomat said that Trump "has placed himself on the wrong side: with the autocrats, the corrupt, and the anti-Americans" (Daniel Fried, quoted in "Trump Attends G-7 with Defiance, Proposing to Readmit Russia," by Michael D. Shear, *The New York Times*, June 8, 2018).

He Met with the World's Two Leading Kims!

June 13, 2018

Globe-trotting Trump ventured out on a limb,
Meeting the murderous dictator Kim.

Grandiose Trump may have acted on whim,
Meeting Kardashian megastar Kim.

Which of these meetings was harder for him?
Which was more perilous, more "sink or swim"?
The one with the woman who shows too much skin,
Or the one with the tyrant who kills his own kin?
Who is more shameless and more self-engrossed?
Who craves attention and ardor the most?
Who is more likely to lie and to boast?
NO, not the Kims . . . *The Apprentice's* host!

～～～～～～～～～～

Trying times call for . . . silly verses (sometimes). Donald Trump met with Kim Jong-un* in Singapore on June 12, 2018, and with Kim Kardashian** at the White House on May 30, 2018. When people glanced at their phones and saw news snippets with the words "Trump" and "Kim," they sometimes couldn't tell which "Kim" would appear in the article. Trump's reality show, *The Apprentice*, boosted his fame and fortune, paving the way for his presidential run. (Ironically, he had once dismissed reality TV as lowbrow entertainment for "bottom feeders.")

* He ordered the killing of his uncle and half-brother.
** She killed it on reality TV.

Hurry Up, Mr. Mueller!

June 15, 2018

Mr. Mueller, what's taking so long?
Is the case you are structuring strong?
Is there something that's not up to par
With the data you've gathered so far?

New York tackled Donald's foundation,
A self-serving organization,
So even though Schneiderman fled,
The inquiry's moving ahead.

Your slump in the most recent polling
Is *not* in the least bit consoling.
Your approval has taken a beating,
Whereas after the Kim Jong-un meeting
The president relished a poll bump.
More people than ever extol Trump!

Though your probe's independent of polling,
Mr. Mueller, it's time to get rolling!

~~~~~~~~~~~~~~~~~~~~~~~~~~~~~~~

Many people were eagerly waiting for—and worrying about—the Mueller report, although more patient (and wiser) minds wanted Mueller to take his time and uncover as much as possible. The New York Attorney General's office, under former Attorney General Eric Schneiderman, had been investigating the Trump Foundation, and on June 14, 2018, about six weeks after Schneiderman resigned in disgrace, his replacement filed a lawsuit accusing the foundation (and members of the Trump family) of more than a decade of "persistent illegal conduct." Meanwhile, after his summit meeting with North Korean dictator Kim Jong-un on June 12, Trump's approval rating went up. Mueller's sank to an all-time low around the same time.

Caged Children
June 19, 2018

A crisis at the border.
An empathy disorder.
Crying kids are torn away.
Tearful parents hope and pray.

Children are in cages!
Trump, however, rages,
"Criminals and thieves!"
Plainly he perceives
Brown skin to be lesser,
Which makes him an oppressor
Of helpless boys and girls.
His policy unfurls,
Devoid of sound analysis.
He glories in its callousness.

"The Democrats deserve the blame,"
He lied without a hint of shame.
But Stephen Miller, Trump, and Sessions
Support these new and harsh oppressions—
Fear of seeming weak and toothless
Makes them inhumane and ruthless.

~~~~~~~~~~~~~~

In April 2018, U.S. Attorney General Jeff Sessions announced a new "zero toler-ance" policy that subjected all adults who cross the Southwest border illegally to *criminal prosecution*, with no exceptions for asylum seekers or parents traveling with children. Previously, most families crossing the border illegally were pro-cessed in *civil* proceedings. As a consequence of this new program, about three thousand children were separated from their parents. Trump falsely blamed Democrats—who were very critical of the separation policy—for obstructing legislation that would fix the situation. Trump advisor Stephen Miller, notorious as an anti-immigration hardliner, was the chief proponent and strongest defender of the new policy. On June 20, after a nationwide outcry, Trump ended the practice of family separation and replaced it with a policy of family detention, while otherwise keeping the zero-tolerance program in place. (In January 2021, in the first week of the Biden administration, the Department of Justice rescinded the zero-tolerance program.)

Donald, Don't Court Chaos!

June 30, 2018

You keep moving to the right,
And we *know* you like to fight
And undo Obama's actions—
But our nation's torn in factions!

Though we know the Court's your call,
Can't you spare us from a brawl?
Merrick Garland as your pick
Would (it's likely) do the trick!

The G.O.P. used to be fine with him.
Why, just ask Orrin Hatch.
The left wing was never aligned with him.
For centrists he's a match.

So please avoid a nasty fight,
Prevent a Congress split with spite.
Choose a thoughtful, prudent jurist,
Not an avid, right-wing purist.

~~~~~~~~~~~~~~~~

Justice Anthony Kennedy's announcement that he would retire at the end of the Supreme Court term on July 31 worried liberals and moderates. Ever since Justice Sandra Day O'Connor retired in 2006, Kennedy had been the swing vote in many of the Court's most divisive decisions, siding, for example, with the liberals in the 2015 case that legalized same-sex marriage, and with the conservatives in the 2013 case that gutted the Voting Rights Act of 1965. Gone were the days when an esteemed judge or lawyer—whether liberal, moderate, or conservative—could be confirmed by a 96-3 vote, as Justice Ruth Bader Ginsburg was in 1993. Republican Senator Orrin Hatch even recommended the liberal Ginsburg to President Clinton. Hatch twice mentioned Merrick Garland, a federal appeals-court judge, as a possible Supreme Court justice, first in 2010, when Elena Kagan was nominated, and even in 2016, just a week before Senate Majority Leader Mitch McConnell (R-KY) announced his plan to deny Obama a court pick. McConnell would not even hold hearings for Obama's choice, Merrick Garland, who was known as a moderate. This poem offered a good suggestion, even though there was no chance Trump would consider it.

Don't F With Our Democracy!

July 17, 2018

Russian boss Putin is having his way.
Useful-fool Donald is such easy prey.
Dependent on Russians for oligarch aid,
Rejected by Wall Street (he never repaid),
He needed the Russians to keep him afloat
And give him a license to brag and to gloat
And feign he was skilled in the "art of the deal,"
When really his tactics were "lie, cheat, and steal."

Russians with money have friends in high places—
They lend overseas and they hardly leave traces.
To *stay* rich they keep in boss Putin's good graces,
And that's a key reason that Donald embraces
The Russians and Putin, and even defaces
His own F.B.I. and its very strong cases
That Russia helped tilt our political races
In favor of Trump and the power he chases.

Interference like this for our country is new—
The election was tainted but what can we do?
We *can't* wave a wand and decree it undone
Or go back in time and then have it re-run.

The tax law, Supreme Court, and E.P.A. gutting,
Plus decades of expertise damaged by cutting—
These far-reaching changes now seem illegitimate.
Republicans, though, very gladly permitted it.
If Trump and his minions don't put country first,
They'll leave our democracy quaking and cursed.

The headlines were clear: "Trump Sides with Russia Against F.B.I. at Helsinki Summit" (BBC) and "Trump's Helsinki Bow to Putin Leaves World Wondering: Why?" (NPR). On July 16, 2018, Trump and Russian President Vladimir Putin held a summit in Helsinki, Finland. It opened with Trump winking at Putin in front of the press. Then the two men met for two hours in private (except for translators), against the advice of senators and other experts (including Republicans). Administration officials were unable to obtain a transcript of the meeting.

In a joint news conference right after the summit, Putin claimed that Russia did *not* interfere with the 2016 election, and—before a baffled world—Trump agreed with him, stating, "President Putin was extremely strong and powerful in his denial today." Top U.S. intelligence officials, however, were certain that Russia had interfered in the election. Democrats were scathing in their denunciation of Trump, with some Republicans joining them. A day after the summit, Trump's own director of national intelligence stated that the intelligence community has "been clear in our assessments of Russian meddling in the 2016 election and their ongoing, pervasive efforts to undermine our democracy." Senator John McCain (R-AZ) called Trump's conduct at the summit "one of the most disgraceful performances" by a U.S. president. Senate Majority Leader Mitch McConnell (R-KY) said he "entirely agree[s] with the assessment of our intelligence community," and Senator Lindsey Graham (R-SC) tweeted that it was a "missed opportunity . . . to firmly hold Russia accountable for 2016 meddling."

Just days before the Helsinki summit, Special Counsel Robert Mueller indicted twelve Russian intelligence officers for hacking into the computer networks of Democratic election organizations and the Hillary Clinton campaign, with the intention of boosting Trump and harming Clinton. No one said out loud that if the Russians had helped Trump win, were his major actions as president somehow "illegitimate"—including his Supreme Court pick (only one at this time), the gutting of the Environmental Protection Agency (E.P.A.), the new tax law, and the loss of expertise at the State Department and elsewhere?

The relationship between Trump and Russia existed long before his presidential run. For example, Trump visited Moscow in July 1987 to discuss real estate and returned with politics in mind. Shortly after the Moscow visit, he spent almost $100,000 for full-page newspaper ads that parroted anti-Western Russian talking points.

Unhinged: Book Tour de Force

August 23, 2018

Omarosa won't care if you love her or hate her,
And Trump would be wise not to *ever* debate her.
She's fearless, well-spoken, dynamic, and strong,
And surely he knows that her claims aren't wrong.
The media loved every juicy leaked morsel.
Her tapes served to prove she was truthful and forceful.
Her hidden but useful and trusty recorder
Supplied us with glimpses of White House disorder.
She triumphed on talk shows, audacious and grand,
And showed to her skeptics her clear upper hand.
She could have spent *weeks* sharing insider views,
But splashier things pulled her book from the news:
The Manafort verdict and Cohen's big plea
Decidedly ended her interview spree.
But she's likely not done with her time on the stage—
She embodies our instant-news, self-obsessed age.
Perhaps she will never be asked onto Fox again,
But—just as with Donald—the limelight's her oxygen.

~~~~~~

Omarosa Manigault Newman, a former communications director in the Trump administration and a contestant on Trump's reality TV show, released a tell-all book, *Unhinged: An Insider's Account of the Trump White House*, in mid-August. In the book, she called Trump a racist and stated that his cognitive functioning was deteriorating. For a short time, Omarosa (she is known by her first name) was omnipresent, and her book topped the *New York Times* bestseller list. She appeared on most of the major TV news shows, and she attracted additional publicity when she leaked secret audio recordings from her White House days. Her time in the spotlight, however, was abruptly cut short: two bigger happenings hit the headlines, both on the same day. First, a jury found former Trump campaign manager Paul Manafort guilty on eight counts of financial crimes, and second, former Trump lawyer Michael Cohen pleaded guilty to eight criminal charges, including tax fraud and campaign-finance violations related to his work for Trump. Omarosa disappeared from the news and her book sales plummeted.

Lodestar

September 6, 2018

An op-ed by someone who dares not be named
Declares a cabal in the White House has tamed
The baser ideas of an amoral man
Who's lacking in wisdom, a vision, or plan.
If *this* is the state of our shaky democracy,
Is it better or worse than a Trump kakistocracy?
We *do* need a lodestar to guide us anew,
But *not* undercover, as one of Trump's crew.

~~~~~~~~~~~~~~~~~~~~~~~~~~~~~~~~~~~~~

On September 5, 2018, an anonymous op-ed appeared in the *New York Times*. "I Am Part of the Resistance Inside the Trump Administration," its headline shouted. The subheading explained: "I work for the president but like-minded colleagues and I have vowed to thwart parts of his agenda and his worst inclinations." The author wrote that "many of the senior officials" in the administration believe that their "first duty is to this country, and the president continues to act in a manner that is detrimental to the health of our republic." He (or she) added that the "root of the problem is the president's amorality." Described only as "a senior official in the Trump administration," the author said that the country needs someone like the late John McCain to serve as a "lodestar for restoring honor to public life and our national dialogue." In October 2020, more than two years later, the author identified himself: at the time of the op-ed, he was deputy chief of staff to the secretary of homeland security, unknown to the general public. Many were disappointed; there had been speculation that the mystery author was a well-known figure in the Trump administration, such as Senior Counselor Kellyanne Conway, Secretary of State Mike Pompeo, or even Vice President Mike Pence (the latter because research indicated that Pence had used the uncommon word "lodestar" in several recent speeches).

Judicial Temperament

September 28, 2018

A petulant, frat-bratty "bro"
Fell short in attempting to show
A demeanor that's suited for judges,
With his resolute, partisan grudges
And retorts full of immature sneers
To the questions on drinking and beers.
The nerve-wracking polarization
Engulfing our worrying nation
Will grow if the G.O.P.'s keen
On backing this overgrown teen.

~~~~~~~~~~~~~~~~~~~~~~~~~~~

Trump nominated Brett Kavanaugh, a judge on a prestigious federal appeals court, to fill Justice Anthony Kennedy's slot on the U.S. Supreme Court. Kennedy had been the swing vote in some of the Court's most controversial cases (see the description with "Donald, Don't Court Chaos!" from June 30, 2018), and Kavanaugh was likely to shift the court further to the right. As a young lawyer, he had worked with Ken Starr on the investigation of President Bill Clinton's relationship with Monica Lewinsky. At the time, Kavanaugh wrote that "going easy" on Clinton in questioning would be "abhorrent," adding that "it is our job to make his pattern of revolting behavior clear—piece by painful piece."

In July, when the media reported that Kavanaugh was on Trump's short list, Christine Blasey Ford, a psychology professor in California, contacted her U.S. congresswoman and senator with allegations that Kavanaugh, "visibly drunk," had sexually assaulted her at a party when they were in high school. Ford did *not* want to be identified, but by September, she and her accusation were known to the public.

Kavanaugh's confirmation hearing on September 27, 2018, was fraught, heated, and contentious. Many observers found Ford, in her testimony, to be "authentic, determined, and also vulnerable," in the words of Maeve Reston of CNN. Kavanaugh, whose denial of the allegation was unequivocal, was, by turns, contemptuous, tearful, petulant, and belligerent. At one point, he explicitly attacked Democrats and abandoned any pretense of displaying judicial, non-partisan equanimity. He also sneered in response to questions. For example, when Senator Sheldon Whitehouse (D-RI) asked about his drinking, Kavanaugh sneered, "I like beer. You like beer? What do you like to drink, Senator?"

The Republicans on the Senate Judiciary Committee coddled and defended Kavanaugh. But not every Republican observer was supportive. Charlie Sykes, a conservative commentator, said, "Even if you support Brett Kavanaugh . . . that was breathtaking as an abandonment of any pretense of having a judicial temperament." Retired Supreme Court Justice John Paul Stevens initially backed Kavanaugh, but changed his mind after watching Kavanaugh's volatility at the hearings.

Unequal Opportunity

October 2, 2018

If a woman had ranted like Senator Graham,
He would've said, "You're hysterical, ma'am."
If a woman had sniveled like hotheaded Brett,
The consensus would be that she's *not* a safe bet
For a slot on the uppermost court of our nation—
They would say she's too *moody* to gain confirmation.
If a woman evaded a senator's question,
The consensus would be that she has no discretion.
If a *man* were as earnest and forthright as Ford,
His disclosures would never be mocked or ignored.

A *man* can act out with astounding impunity.
Will women one day have the same opportunity?

During his confirmation hearings, Brett Kavanaugh was emotional and teary, without the dignity and composure one might expect from a judge. He shouted in response to some of Senator Dianne Feinstein's (D-CA) questions without actually answering her. He displayed a startling lack of respect to Senator Amy Klobuchar (D-MN) after she explained that she was familiar with alcohol abuse because her father had been an alcoholic. "Have you ever blacked out?" she asked. Kavanaugh snarled in response, "Have you?" In contrast, Christine Blasey Ford was poised and firm in her testimony. Kavanaugh found a sympathetic advocate in Senator Lindsey Graham (R-SC), who railed against the Democrats in a surprisingly histrionic speech.

If a woman had displayed Graham's emotional intensity and melodrama—or Kavanaugh's combination of self-pity, hostility, and tears—would Republicans welcome her into the halls of power?

Squirrel Hill Synagogue: Absence of Empathy
October 28, 2018

When eleven from Pittsburgh were brutally slain,
He complained that his hairdo got mussed in the rain.
Of *course* we're aware of his dear Jewish daughter,
But still, on the day of the Squirrel Hill slaughter,
Instead of a message to soothe and to mourn,
He blasted, with vehement anger and scorn,
The "caravan," Clinton, the press, CNN . . .
When what he said should have been "Never again."

~~~~~~~~~~~~~~~~~~~~~~~~~~~

On October 27, 2018, a gunman murdered eleven worshipers at the Tree of Life Synagogue in the Squirrel Hill neighborhood of Pittsburgh. He claimed that Jews were helping to transport a migrant "caravan" from Central America, a group that Trump had been hyping as an invasion and a threat to American security. A couple of hours before the massacre, the gunman posted a sinister message on a right-wing chat site: "HIAS likes to bring invaders in that kill our people. I can't sit by and watch my people get slaughtered. . . . I'm going in." (HIAS, the Hebrew Immigrant Aid Society, helps refugees of all religions, nationalities, and ethnic groups.) The caravan was actually a group of refugees fleeing violence in their home countries.

What was Trump's response to the synagogue murders? He joked that he almost canceled an event because, after having to speak to reporters in the rain about the shooting, he was having "a bad hair day." Only after his Jewish daughter and son-in-law implored him did Trump issue a powerful statement against anti-Semitism. Later on the day of the synagogue murders, Trump appeared at a rally. At first he tried to "tone it down," but it didn't take long for him to start riling up his audience with attacks on CNN, the "caravan," Hillary Clinton, and Representative Maxine Waters (D-CA). Because the two women had been targets of pipe bombs sent by a vocal Trump supporter just a few days earlier, his shouted attacks on them were yet another display of his incivility.

Midterms: Blue Wave or Blue Mood?

November 7, 2018

So, *was* it a blue wave or merely a puddle?
A pivotal shift or a multi-part muddle?
Gutsy Beto was close but it wasn't enough—
Shifting Texas to blue will be tricky and tough.
Also, Heidi and Claire in their solid red states
Suffered sad but completely foreseeable fates.
The House grew more blue but the Senate more red,
Meaning Trump as a force is a long way from dead.
Yet a dastardly, slippery slide to autocracy
Was thwarted (for now) by an active democracy. . . .

~~~~~~~~~~~~~~~~~~~~~~~~~~~~

Results of the 2018 midterm elections were mixed. The Democrats made a net gain of forty-one seats in the House, achieving a majority and ending Republican control of the chamber. The Republicans retained control of the Senate, with a net gain of two seats and the defeat of four Democratic incumbents—including Heidi Heitkamp of North Dakota and Claire McCaskill of Missouri—from states that voted for Trump in 2016. Democrat Beto O'Rourke, then a U.S. Representative, mounted a long-shot challenge to Senator Ted Cruz in deep-red Texas. Cruz won, but O'Rourke performed well and was probably responsible for several Democratic down-ticket victories in the state. The Democrats' newfound majority in the House put an end to the Republican "trifecta"—their control of the presidency, Senate, and House.

Callous Malice

November 12, 2018

Homes—destroyed. People—dead.
Fires roared and thousands fled.
Responders battled. Forests died.
"But YOU'RE to blame," our "leader" cried.
"Mismanaged lands—fix that now!
Or pretty soon I won't allow
Disaster aid to go your way.
Correct it NOW or I won't pay!"
Fires, slaughters, hurricanes—
The grieving are the ones he blames.

⁓⁓⁓⁓⁓⁓⁓⁓⁓⁓⁓⁓⁓

Horrific wildfires in California killed more than one hundred people and burned nearly two million acres. Trump blamed the fires on state forest mismanagement and threatened to withhold federal aid for the victims and communities. He tweeted, "There is no reason for these massive, deadly and costly forest fires in California except that forest management is so poor. . . . Remedy now, or no more Fed payments!"

Trump was incorrect to blame *state* forest management; many of the worst fires were on *federal* land. In addition, even though forest management was a factor, more pertinent causes included high winds, drought resulting from climate change, and badly managed Pacific Gas and Electric power lines.

Whatever the causes of the catastrophe, a less heartless president would have shown compassion for people who their lost homes or loved ones, and for the firefighters battling the blazes. Trump was similarly insensitive after the Pittsburgh synagogue shooting when he seemed to fault the victims and grieving congregants, musing that if the synagogue had hired an armed guard, the murders would have been prevented. The year before, Trump blamed Puerto Ricans for their territory's slow recovery from Hurricane Maria, after people complained that his administration's response was inadequate. (Later, an inspector general's report found that the Trump administration had obstructed and delayed more than twenty billion dollars in hurricane relief to the territory.)

"No One Told Me" (Duh!)

November 20, 2018

Riddle:

After endless hype and fervor
Over Clinton's private server,
GUESS who used a private email?
Here's a hint: a high-up female.

Answer:

It's IVANKA, Trump's "advisor,"
Someone who you'd think was wiser.

Solution:

Lock her up and take the key—
She'll do time with Hillary!

An "oops" for the First Daughter. Donald Trump, as everyone knows, led fevered chants of "lock her up" at his campaign rallies, in reference to Hillary Clinton and her use of a private email system while she was secretary of state. It was thus surprising when Ivanka Trump was discovered doing something similar. On November 19, 2018, the *Washington Post* reported that Ivanka had used a personal email account to send hundreds of emails pertaining to official government matters, many in violation of federal records requirements. She told White House lawyers that she was not aware of breaking any email rules. Really? At minimum, after her father's frenzy over Clinton's emails, Ivanka should have been more concerned about using a personal email account in her capacity as a presidential advisor. She could have sought out guidance, if no one had explained the rules to her. (Ivanka, however, did *not* set up a private email server in her home, as Hillary Clinton did for both work and personal emails when she was secretary of state.)

Lies, Lies, and More Lies

December 1, 2018

Manafort and Cohen lied!
Surely they have lots to hide.

Manafort was Donald's mole
In Mueller's probe—a slimy role.

Wretched Cohen now reveals
Trump was keen on Russian deals!

In secret, Trump conferred with Stone,
Who blithely told him on the phone,
"WikiLeaks is gonna dump
Emails that will *help* you, Trump—
Emails filched from Clinton backers,
Thanks to clever Russian hackers!"

My brain is dazed, my mind might crack—
This plot's too thick; I can't keep track.
But I have reached a sound conclusion:
Chicanery, if not collusion.

~~~~~~~~~~~~~~~~~~~~~

The last few days of November were disconcerting. Special Counsel Robert Mueller's office revealed that Paul Manafort, Trump's former campaign chairman, violated his plea agreement, signed two months earlier, by lying repeatedly to Mueller's team. In addition, while Manafort was "cooperating" with Mueller, Manafort's attorneys were disclosing details about the investigation to Trump's legal team. We also learned that Michael Cohen, Trump's former lawyer, lied to Congress about the timing of the negotiations to build a tower in Moscow. Trump, through Cohen, was involved in and apprised of the negotiations deep into the presidential campaign (if not throughout it), well beyond the point originally acknowledged. This meant that the Moscow real estate deal was still under discussion at the time of the infamous Trump Tower meeting, in June 2016, between a well-connected Russian lawyer and Trump's top campaign aides, who hoped to receive damaging information on Hillary Clinton. It also shows that Trump, while running for president and denying links to Russia, was, in fact, pursuing a large real estate deal that likely depended on help from the Russian government. In addition, new evidence emerged that political trickster Roger Stone, a longtime Trump advisor, knew in advance that WikiLeaks was planning to reveal another round of Russian-hacked Democratic emails to hurt Hillary Clinton. The day after Stone learned about the upcoming email dump, he spoke privately to Trump on the phone. Stone, however, claimed that the subject of the hacked emails never came up. Was that too a lie?

Pelosi: 2019 Preview?

December 13, 2018

Pelosi:
We know she
Will show she
Grasps how to think
Tactically
Practically
She's *not* one to shrink.

She'll negotiate
Tell it straight
And stand up to Trump.

She's forceful
Resourceful
And never a chump.

Watch closely—
Pelosi
Knows what she's doing.

The G.O.P.
Instinctively
Knows trouble's brewing.

~~~~~~~~~~~~~~~~~~~~~~~~

On December 11, 2018, U.S. Representative Nancy Pelosi (D-CA) and Senator Chuck Schumer (D-NY) met with Trump in the Oval Office to discuss the president's threat to shut down the government unless he got $5.6 billion in congressional funding for a border wall. The meeting, which Pelosi and Schumer thought would be private, turned into televised political theater because Trump insisted that it be aired. That turned out to be no problem for Pelosi: she demonstrated that she was fully capable of taking on Trump. (The Democrats had just won a majority in the House, and Pelosi was likely to be Speaker.) After the meeting, Pelosi strutted out of the White House wearing sunglasses and a stylish brick-red coat, radiating energy and power. Some wondered whether the meeting was a preview of the drama to come in 2019.

Petulant Policy

December 20, 2018

"I like to prove I'm big and tough!
But having bone spurs sure was rough.
OUT of Syria, OUT we go!
Though the generals told me NO!
They said my order hurts the Kurds
But *I* don't need those four-star nerds.
A stable genius doesn't need
Advice from generals to succeed.
Border troops—my midterm ruse—
Also bypassed 'expert' views.
I'M the boss and I will show it!
AND I never, ever blow it."
(Yes, he does, but doesn't know it.)

~~~~~~~~~~~~~~~~~~~~~~~~~~~~~~~

Trump had no military experience. He dodged service in the Vietnam War with dubious claims of "bone spurs" (thus putting the "spur" in "spurious"). He nonetheless presented himself as "knowing more than the generals." To prove it, he made two decisions in late 2018 that were widely deplored by actual military professionals. On December 19, 2018, Trump suddenly announced that he planned to withdraw U.S. troops from Syria, against the advice of his own generals and civilian advisors. Military leaders denounced Trump's plan, explaining that it would likely lead to a rebound of ISIS in the region and, even worse, betray the U.S.'s Syrian Kurdish allies, who had done the bulk of the fighting against ISIS. Prominent members of Trump's own party—including Senators Mitch McConnell (R-KY), Marco Rubio (R-FL), and Lindsey Graham (R-SC)—agreed with the military experts. The next day, after failing to convince Trump to reconsider, Secretary of Defense James Mattis, a four-star general, resigned. The other ill-conceived decision came in the run-up to the midterm elections, when Trump sent nearly six thousand active-duty troops to the border with Mexico to "protect" the U.S. from a "caravan" of immigrants he claimed was "invading" the country. Blaming Democrats for this "danger," he sought to rile up anti-immigrant voters. In truth, the caravan consisted of refugees, mostly from Honduras, fleeing violence in their home country, and they were at least a month away from the border. Military leaders called Trump's use of troops a "political stunt" and a "wasteful deployment" that violated the American principle of keeping the Army out of politics. (Once the midterm elections were over, Trump barely mentioned the "caravan" again. In all likelihood, he knew it was a non-existent threat.)

Dow Downer

December 21, 2018

The Dow is down to twenty-two,
And *hell*, we don't know what to do!
Will stopping Donald's tariff war
Allow our stocks to rouse and soar?
Can Mattis un-resign and wait
Till global market fears abate?
The Nasdaq's now in *bear* terrain,
Demolishing its former gain.
The Fed is raising rates anew—
And surely that's a factor too.
With D.C. deadlocked—shutdown fears—
The Dow drop was the worst in years.

~~~~~~~~~~~~~~~~~~~~~~~~~~~~~~~~~~~~~~

December 2018 was a terrible month for the stock market, with the major indices hitting new lows for the year. On Friday, December 21, the Dow Jones Industrial Average suffered its worse week since the financial crisis in 2008, falling more than 400 points and closing below 22,500. The Nasdaq closed in a bear market, and the S&P 500 was at the edge of bear territory.

Several factors contributed to the decline. One was Trump's tariff war with China ("A careless China tariff tweet / And *boom*, the market's in retreat.") Political infighting in D.C. was also a negative, especially Trump's threat of a government shutdown if he didn't get funding for his Mexican border wall. Concerns about a global economic slowdown added to Wall Street's anxiety, as did the Federal Reserve's rate hike, on December 19, to its highest level since the spring of 2008. The surprise resignation of Defense Secretary James Mattis on December 20 also rattled investors—he was a solace to many on Wall Street who viewed him as a "serious adult" in the chaotic Trump administration. These factors, combined with Trump's recent volatility, made investors nervous.

2019

In 2019, the G.O.P. became increasingly Trump-centric, even as their leader made decisions that many of his top allies and advisors opposed. At the urging of Turkish strongman Recep Erdogan, Trump defied his military advisors and withdrew U.S. troops from Syria, paving the way for a Turkish military assault on the Syrian Kurds, who had been staunch U.S. allies in the fight against ISIS. At home, the Mueller report—the culmination of the Special Counsel investigation into Russian interference in the 2016 election—was finally released, having first been dishonestly summarized by U.S. Attorney General William Barr. After evading serious scrutiny for years, Jeffrey Epstein, a well-connected financier with an unclear source of wealth, was arrested for sex trafficking of minors in a sordid saga with a sidebar that included the resignation of a Trump Cabinet member. On a brighter note, more than two dozen men and women—the most diverse field in history—entered the campaign for the Democratic Party's nomination for president. The most significant news of 2019 was the impeachment inquiry into Trump for soliciting foreign interference in the 2020 presidential election to harm a political rival. As the inquiry found, Trump withheld congressionally authorized military aid from Ukraine to pressure Ukraine's new president, Volodymyr Zelensky, to announce an investigation into Joe Biden and his son. In December, the House voted in favor of impeachment, largely along party lines.

Congresscreature Steve King of Iowa

January 16, 2019

"What's wrong with white supremacy?
Why can't you give me clemency?
I've been in Congress many years.
I'm innocent of slurs and smears!"

He's clueless, racist, unaware.
His colleagues finally stripped him bare,
Removing him from high positions
And halting his malign ambitions.

"Go find another job," said Mitch.
That's nice, but here's the glaring hitch:
Steve King for *years* was in the wrong.
So what took Congress so damn long?

~~~~~~~~~~~~~~~~~~~~~~~~~~~~~~~~~~~~~

In a *New York Times* interview published in January 2019, U.S. Representative Steve King (R-IA) questioned why white supremacy and white nationalism are considered offensive. Afterward, many prominent Republicans denounced King. Senate Majority Leader Mitch McConnell (R-KY) said that King "should find another line of work," and Senator Mitt Romney (R-UT) suggested that King resign. On January 14, House Republican leaders removed King from his committee assignments. King had a long history of making racist statements, and it was unclear why congressional Republicans didn't act earlier to curtail him. He lost his next election.

Priorities

February 16, 2019

Trump's latest tweet (not really):

"A national emergency!
A heightened sense of urgency!
I'll set the tone as head of state,
But, gee, my golf game just can't wait."

~~~~~~~~~~~~~~~~~~~~~~~~~~~~~~~~~~~~~~

On February 15, 2019, after Congress declined to approve the funding Trump wanted for his Mexican border wall, he declared a national emergency in an attempt to bypass Congress and access billions of dollars already appropriated for other programs. How dire was the emergency? It was so dire that, later that same day, he flew to his Palm Beach home to spend the weekend playing golf. Many pundits and politicians (including some Republicans) denounced the emergency as "fake"—a made-up crisis by a dishonest president desperate for a political win. The constitutionality of his declaration was also in question. The *New York Times* editorial board called Trump's action "a breathtaking display of executive disregard for the separation of powers, [with] the White House . . . thumbing its nose at Congress." Later, Trump more or less admitted that there was no emergency. "I didn't need to do this," he said, adding that he just wanted to get the wall done "much faster."

Mueller Report
(*Limerick*)

March 23, 2019

Yes, the Mueller report is now *out*!
Will it please us or leave us in doubt?
Will it sow vast confusion
Or show past collusion,
And give Democrats muscle and clout?

Yet we wonder, will Barr let us see it?
As of now, he will *not* guarantee it.
But the full-length report
Is of such great import
That Barr, we implore you to free it!

We aren't quite sure he'll agree,
No matter the strength of our plea,
But can *that* be okay?
And does Barr's D.O.J.
Work for Trump, or for you and for me?

~~~~~~~~~~~~~~~~~~~~~

On March 22, 2019, Special Counsel Robert Mueller delivered his long-awaited report to Attorney General William Barr, after an almost two-year investigation into (a) Russia's efforts to interfere in the 2016 U.S. presidential election, (b) possible coordination or collusion between Russian agents and Trump's campaign associates, and (c) possible obstruction of justice by Trump. The next day, Barr and his team scrutinized the 448-page report, discussing how to present its findings and how much of it to release. Many wanted Barr to release the report in its entirety, not only to Congress but also to the public. Barr's role as attorney general was to represent the American public, not to protect Trump, but Barr often acted as if he were the president's personal attorney.

BarrStool Talk

March 25, 2019

Republicans: There's not enough to charge obstruction!
Democrats: We wanna make our own deduction!

Rs: But Trump is now *exonerated*!
Ds: You clearly have exaggerated.

Ds: We wanna read the full report!
Rs: We think it's *fine* Barr kept it short.

Ds: His letter's just defensive spin.
Rs: You're just upset you failed to win.

Ds: But Trump's campaign team *talked* with Russians!
Rs: But no collusion, just discussions.

Ds: But they requested Clinton smut!
Rs: An easy ask; there's *such* a glut.

Ds: The House is still investigating!
Rs: That Adam Schiff is irritating.

Ds: This surely isn't over yet!
Rs: But *we* will win. You wanna bet?

Rs: And party warfare, that's our strength!
Ds: To win, you'll go to *any* length.

Rs: We're *far* more skilled at this than you.
Ds: But what you say is seldom true.

~~~~~~~~~~~~~~~~~~~~~~~~~~~~~~~~~

On March 24, 2019, Attorney General William Barr released a "summary" of
the Mueller report in a letter to the House and Senate Judiciary Committees.
Barr's letter soft-pedaled Mueller's findings on Russian contacts with Trump's

campaign team and the president's possible obstruction of justice. As a result, Republicans claimed "victory," with Democrats demanding to know more. The House Intelligence Committee, with Adam Schiff (D-CA) as chair, was still investigating Trump's connections to Russia, apart from Special Counsel Mueller's probe. (After the release of the redacted Mueller report in mid-April, many legal analysts and journalists denounced Barr's letter, stating that it intentionally misrepresented the report's conclusions to shape pubic opinion and protect Trump. At the end of April, the public learned that on March 27, 2019, Mueller himself had written to Barr, objecting to Barr's summary because it "did not fully capture the context, nature, and substance of [the Special Counsel's] work and conclusions.")

G.O.P. to U.S.A.: We Really Don't Care!
March 28, 2019

"The Special Olympics—we'll slash their support!
Affordable Care Act—we'll take it to court!
Pre-existing conditions, we DON'T give a hoot!
And disabled young athletes, we'll give you the boot!
Safe food and clean water and breathable air?
Yes, we and our industry donors don't CARE!
If you or your children ingest toxic waste,
It's just a forgettable, minor distaste.
The common good's something that's not in our zone.
For health and well-being, you're all on your own."

~~~~~~~~~~~~~~~~~~~~~~~~~~~~~

Trump's budget proposal for the 2020 fiscal year called for increased military spending, funding for the border wall with Mexico, and deep cuts for education, Medicare, Medicaid, and environmental programs, including a reduction of 31% for the Environmental Protection Agency. The Department of Education proposed a cut of nearly $18 million for the Special Olympics, which operates a school program that promotes social inclusion by bringing together students with and without disabilities. (After a bipartisan outcry, Trump reversed course on the Special Olympics funding cuts.) Also in March, the Department of Justice (D.O.J.) asked an appeals court to invalidate the entire Affordable Care Act (A.C.A.). Earlier, the D.O.J. had declined to defend the A.C.A.'s protections for people with preexisting conditions. (The title of the poem is a reference to the jacket Melania Trump wore to and from her visit to migrant children in Texas.)-

Time to Dis Barr

April 21, 2019

My dear Mister Barr,
You've gone much too far
In a wrongful direction.
You've abused your discretion!
Why, even Jeff Sessions
Absorbed civics lessons!
Though Sessions was awful,
He knew it's unlawful
For the U.S.A.G.
To behave as if he
Were counsel for POTUS.
So here is your notice:
The oath that you swore
(And chose to ignore)
Says those in your station
Shall serve our great nation!

Again, just in case you forgot:
Your role very clearly is not
To protect the Commander in Chief,
In spite of his wayward belief.
So don't be a toady or chump—
Your client is not Donald Trump!
Your client's the whole U.S.A.,
So please start behaving that way!

~~~~~~~~~~~~~~~~~~~~~~~~~~~~~~~~~~~~~~

The Department of Justice released a redacted version of the Mueller report on April 18, 2019. Political analysts compared it to Attorney General William Barr's letter summarizing the report and concluded that the letter was a deliberate mischaracterization of Mueller's findings. Barr's letter omitted key information and took phrases out of context to make the report seem more favorable to Trump. (See the description accompanying "BarrStool Talk," March 25, 2019.)

Trump apparently thought the role of the U.S. attorney general (U.S.A.G.) was to protect the president, when, in truth, the A.G.'s job is to represent the United States and the American people. Jeff Sessions, the first senator to endorse Trump, was rewarded with the position of attorney general. Session recused himself from the probe into Russian interference in the 2016 election because he had been an advisor to Trump's campaign team and had met with the Russian ambassador to the U.S. in the course of the campaign. Sessions explained that his recusal was consistent with "the rule of law" and "the integrity that's required of the attorney general." Trump was angry that he did not have a loyal protector overseeing the inquiry and furious that Sessions had recused himself. Trump pressured Sessions to change his mind, but Sessions declined. Ultimately, Sessions resigned as attorney general, at Trump's request, in early November 2018. In early December, Trump nominated William Barr to succeed Sessions. Few were surprised at Trump's choice. In June 2018, Barr, then a lawyer in private practice, had submitted an unsolicited nineteen-page memo to the Justice Department, criticizing Mueller's investigation and arguing that a president cannot obstruct justice as a matter of law when he is exercising executive power. In February 2019, Barr was confirmed in a near party-line vote. In the words of Charles Pierce of *Esquire* magazine, Barr "did what he was hired to do," as evidenced by his letter minimizing Mueller's findings.

Beseech to Impeach?

May 30, 2019

If we impeach him,
What would it teach him. . . .

He still won't know
Right from wrong.

His base will grow
Far too strong.

Pelosi opposes
These drastic actions.

The Dems have now split
Into further factions.

We're damned if we don't
And damned if we do.

If only we knew
What will ensue.

~~~~~~~~~~~~~~~~~~~

After the release of the Mueller report, some House Democrats called for Trump to be impeached, but others counseled against it. House Speaker Nancy Pelosi (D-CA) wanted to continue the investigations that had already begun, instead of pursing impeachment. After Special Counsel Robert Mueller spoke to the press about his report for the first time (May 29, 2019) and refused to clear Trump of criminal wrongdoing, calls for impeachment intensified. In his press briefing, Mueller said that charging Trump with obstruction of justice was "not an option," pursuant to the Department of Justice's policy against prosecuting a sitting president. Mueller noted, however, that if the Special Counsel's team "had confidence that the president clearly did not commit a crime, we would have said that." Amid the growing support from House Democrats for impeachment, Pelosi stuck by her original assertion that it was not the right move, at least not at that time.

Biden, Your Time?

June 23, 2019

Biden, Biden, we've been thinking,
Will your polling soon be sinking?

————

With easy charm and killer smile,
You've stayed in public life awhile.

Your warmth and geniality
Trump Donald's crass venality.

The last time, Joe, you would've won
But Clinton Inc. derailed your run.

You flourished as Obama's mate
But now you might be out of date.

Your Hyde Amendment flip is new—
We're hazy on your point of view.

And lauding your rapport with racists
Displays a certain mental stasis.

YET

Your knowledge and your expertise
Are crucial strengths in times like these.
Your name is known and that does count,
But *can* you gracefully surmount
Your foot-in-mouth deficiencies
And showcase your proficiencies?

In mid-June, polls showed Joe Biden ahead of the other Democratic candidates, with, on average, about 33% favoring him, followed by 15% for Senator

Bernie Sanders (I-VT) and 11% for Senator Elizabeth Warren (D-MA). Earlier in the month, Biden had reversed his longtime support for the Hyde Amendment, which bans federal funding for abortion. Pro-choice Democratic voters, although pleased, were concerned about his mixed record on the issue. Later in June, when touting his ability to work with legislators with whom he disagreed, Biden mentioned two segregationist Southern senators as examples. Many political analysts thought his comment was out of touch and offensive, and they wondered whether it would hurt him. Even so, Biden's name recognition, experience, and empathy worked in his favor.

Topics and Optics: Democratic Debate #1

June 26, 2019

We heard with growing consternation
Competing views on immigration.

All find climate change a threat
(Something Trump will never get).

Single payer? Public option?
Which of these deserves adoption?

Iranian uranium
Has stupefied my cranium.

Some are centrist; others, left.
Who has presidential heft?
Which of them's the safest bet?
No one has impressed me yet.

~~~~~~~~~~~~~~~~~~~~~~~~~~~~~~~

The first Democratic debate of the 2020 campaign season was on June 26, 2019, with ten candidates on stage (out of twenty qualifiers—the other ten participated in a debate the next day). The topics were wide-ranging: immigration, climate change, healthcare, the Iran nuclear deal, and more. The contenders agreed on many issues, but not all. No one engaged in personal attacks; their disagreements were on substantive issues.

The candidates denounced Trump's immigration policies, but they clashed on possible reforms, with Julián Castro criticizing Beto O'Rourke in an intense exchange. The candidates all thought it was a mistake for Trump to withdraw from the Iran nuclear deal, but they differed somewhat on what to do next. Senator Amy Klobuchar (D-MN), like most of the others, said she would rejoin the deal, but she criticized the limited duration of some of the restrictions on Iran's nuclear program, pointing out that Iran was threatening to "blow the caps" on enriching uranium. On healthcare, some called for a single-payer national system, while others preferred an optional public plan. In short, the candidates divided into a progressive group and a more moderate one, while agreeing in general terms on the problems facing the country and the need to defeat Donald Trump.

Sordid and Unreported
(But Worth It to Unearth It)
July 13, 2019

Heads of state and socialites
Mixed at Epstein's dinner nights
With C.E.O.s and finance "bros,"
Who now may face some legal woes.

Acosta's team was sly and sleazy,
Allowing Jeff to get off easy,
And even though his crimes were sordid,
His secret plea went unreported.

A journalist who wouldn't rest—
A free press at its very best—
Pursued and delved with focused zeal,
Exposing Epstein's cushy deal.

And now we see a fouler mess
With Jeff unlikely to confess,
His ties to power quickly fraying,
And men—his "houseguests"—scared and praying.

~~~~~~~~~~~~~~~~~~~~~~~~~~

Sex offender Jeffery Epstein, despicable and inexplicable, was able to live lavishly after a cushy 2008 plea deal in Florida and a short, lenient sentence that he completed in 2009. He continued to mingle in high places, inviting politicians, celebrities, and financial executives to dinners at his 51,000-square-foot home in Manhattan. In 2017, an intrepid *Miami Herald* reporter, Julie K. Brown, started investigating Epstein, tracking down dozens of women who said he sexually abused or raped them when they were teenagers. In a series of *Miami Herald* articles in November 2018, she revealed the full story behind the lenient 2008 plea deal. Epstein's lawyers negotiated it with Alexander Acosta, then the head federal prosecutor in southern Florida and, at the time of Brown's reporting, Trump's secretary of labor. Acosta agreed to keep the plea deal secret from the victims, in violation of federal law. The deal, a "non-prosecution agreement," gave Epstein and four accomplices immunity from all federal criminal charges, putting an end to an ongoing F.B.I. investigation into additional Epstein victims and prominent adults who may have engaged in Epstein-related sex crimes. As part of the deal, Epstein pleaded guilty to just two state-level sex offenses. He served only thirteen months of his eighteen-month sentence, most of it spent not in a state prison, but in a minimum-security facility in Palm Beach County. At one point, his unit in the facility was kept unlocked, and for most of the sentence, he was free to go to his office twelve hours a day, six days a week, on "work release." More than a decade later, in July 2019, about eight months after the *Miami Herald* articles, Epstein was arrested for sex trafficking of minors in New York and Florida. Soon afterward, Acosta resigned as secretary of labor. About a month after this poem, Epstein was found dead in his jail cell, an apparent suicide.

Crime Bill

August 2, 2019

Long ago and far away,
When Ronald Reagan ruled the day,
The Democrats were running scared,
And so they had to show they cared
'Bout family values, crime, and drugs,
And law and order, gangs and thugs,
Or else they'd lose forevermore
The "Reagan Dems" they had before.

Throughout the eighties crime was rising,
And thus it wasn't so surprising
That by the nineties Congress passed
A brand new crime bill, harsh and vast,
A bill that even liberals lauded,
And city activists applauded,
Mayors, pastors, urbanites
Seeking cures to city blights.
Some in Congress had objections,
Yet it passed with few defections.

Harris said the crime bill shook her,
But she and also Cory Booker
Should look at history again,
For had they been in Congress then,
They may have even voted for it—
With hindsight's ease, they now deplore it.

~~~~~~~~~~~~~~~~~~~~

The sweeping crime bill of 1994 was coming back to haunt Biden. In the second Democratic debate, Senators Cory Booker and Kamala Harris, the two Black candidates in the crowded Democratic field, attacked Biden for his support of the 1994 bill, which many experts now view as a major cause of mass incarceration and injustice. Booker and Harris were trying to portray Biden as out of touch with the current thinking of the Democratic party. Yet Bernie Sanders (who in 1994 was in the House) and many other liberals and progressives voted for the bill—including Senators Russ Feingold, Dianne Feinstein, John Kerry, Chuck Schumer, Representative Kweisi Mfume, and the majority of the Congressional Black Caucus. In addition, many Black mayors and clergymen favored it. Some in Congress voted for it reluctantly, perhaps fearing a harsher bill that lacked funding for prevention and deterrence. Representatives John Lewis (D-GA) and Maxine Waters (D-CA) voted *against* it, showing insight and foresight, rather than the hindsight through which many criticize the act today. The bill drew support for a variety of reasons: crime had been rising, people of all races wanted safe communities, and liberal white politicians wanted to regain their formerly reliable white working-class voters, who had become known as "Reagan Democrats."

Shopping List

August 17, 2019

"I'm going on a shopping spree
And buying things for me me me!
I need a few more long red ties,
And longer-lasting orange dyes,
A golf course here, a building there,
A condo tower near Red Square,
A newly shot and stuffed bald eagle
(Which I decree is not illegal).
Who gives a hoot if that's taboo. . . .
And maybe I'll buy Greenland, too!
It's big and unexploited still.
Let's mine and strip, extract and drill!"

But Denmark says, "It's not for sale!
Your dealmaker skills are stale,
And maybe we'll buy YOU instead!
Your country'd come out well ahead,
With better healthcare, transit, schools—
Hey, U.S.A. . . . Denmark rules!"

~~~~~~~~~~~~~~~~~~~~~~~~

In mid-August 2019, the *Wall Street Journal* reported that Donald Trump was contemplating buying Greenland for the United States. He was impressed with its abundant natural resources. Many laughed at Trump's idea, but Denmark and Greenland (an autonomous country within the Kingdom of Denmark) were not amused. They made it clear that Greenland was not for sale, with the Danish prime minister calling the notion "absurd." Trump said her comment was "nasty" and canceled his upcoming visit to Denmark, a longtime ally. On the domestic front around the same time, the Trump administration announced sweeping changes to the Endangered Species Act (E.S.A.), rolling back protections for wildlife in favor of corporate interests. The E.S.A., signed into law by President Nixon in 1973, is credited with saving the bald eagle—the emblem of the United States since 1782—from extinction.

A Perfectly Normal Phone Call
September 25, 2019

Not having learned from the Mueller report,
Trump said to Zelensky, "Now be a good sport
And get dirt on the Bidens, both father and son,
Or your package of aid will be over and done!"

It was too much for Nancy Pelosi to bear,
But the G.O.P. leaders, of course, did not care.
"My phone call was normal," he said with a shrug.
That's true; he's *accustomed* to being a *thug*!

~~~~~~~~~~~~~~~~~~~~~~

On the heels of the Mueller report on Russian interference in the *prior* election on Trump's behalf, Trump pressured *another* nation to interfere in the *next* election on his behalf. As the public learned in mid-September 2019, Trump, in a phone call two months earlier, made an offer he thought Ukrainian President Volodymyr Zelensky couldn't refuse: Trump would "unfreeze" nearly $400 million in congressionally mandated military aid to Ukraine, if Zelensky would announce that his government was conducting an investigation into Joe Biden—Trump's likely opponent in the 2020 presidential race—and Biden's son, Hunter. Trump also withheld a promised White House meeting in his attempt to coerce Zelensky. At least a week before the phone call, Trump had blocked the already-appropriated aid.

White House staffers, national security advisors, and experts on Ukraine were on the call. A few weeks later, a whistleblower filed a complaint raising concerns about Trump's troubling statements to Zelensky. The result was an impeachment inquiry initiated by Speaker of the House Nancy Pelosi on September 24, 2019. Trump said he did nothing wrong; he claimed that his call with the Ukrainian president was "normal" and legitimate, even "perfect." (Another way to put it: "On his 'perfect' Ukraine call / He had the wanton, heedless gall / To offer up a quid pro quo / To undermine his rival Joe.")

International Relations
October 14, 2019

Erdogan and Putin laughed: "Trump's obedient and daft!"

———

Putin found a perfect putz,
A narcissist who's also nuts,
A pseudo-master of the deal
Whose praise for Putin is surreal.

Turkey too outwitted Trump,
Proving he's a clueless chump.
Our Kurdish allies were betrayed
When Turkey bombed them, unafraid.

In a recent little chat,
Autocrat to autocrat,
Erdogan and Putin smirked,
"Our global plan has clearly worked!
With smooth and easy subterfuge,
Donald Trump's become our stooge."

〜〜〜〜〜〜〜〜〜〜〜〜〜〜

From the beginning of his presidency, Trump expressed admiration for autocrats around the world and even deferred to them. A prominent example: his submissive behavior toward Russia's Vladimir Putin at their 2018 summit meeting in Helsinki. (See the description with the poem "Don't F With Our Democracy," July 17, 2018). Thus it should not have been particularly surprising when Trump, soon after a phone call on October 6, 2019, with Turkish strongman Recep Erdogan, heeded Erdogan's advice over the U.S. military's and withdrew U.S. troops from northern Syria. (Trump had previously, in December 2018, announced his intention to pull American forces from Syria, stunning his national security advisors and causing his secretary of defense to resign. See the description with the poem "Petulant Policy," December 20, 2018.) Trump's order cleared the way for Erdogan to assault the Kurds, who had been vital American allies in the fight against the Islamic State (ISIS) in Syria. Trump's decision drew strong criticism from both Democratic and Republican lawmakers, including Senator Lindsey Graham (R-SC), who usually backed Trump. Officials at the Pentagon, State Department, and White House were also appalled at Trump's betrayal of the Kurds. Putin, however, approved of the move. Erdogan lost no time: a couple of days after Trump pulled the U.S. troops, Turkey launched airstrikes and ground attacks against the Kurds. Some of Trump's own appointees and senior advisors observed that he was "often outplayed in his conversations with powerful leaders like Russian President Vladimir Putin and Turkish President Recep Erdogan," as journalist Carl Bernstein wrote on cnn.com.

His Favorite Things

November 1, 2019

Penthouses, power, and plutocrat nations,
Rallies with cheering and standing ovations,
Big brassy buildings and homes fit for kings,
These are a few of his favorite things.

Girls in low necklines and eye-candy dresses,
Towering heels and long flowing tresses,
Diamonds that dazzle and clothing that clings,
These are a few of his favorite things.

When the press bites, when the *Times* stings,
When he's feeling mad,
He'll simply remember his favorite things,
And then he won't feel so bad.

Conflicts and chaos and selfish corruption,
Falsehoods and flare-ups, a Twitter eruption,
Favors for fawners that come with tight strings,
These are a few of his favorite things.

Putty for Russia and fodder for Turkey—
Links to their leaders are furtive and murky.
They may have sway in his policy swings—
Donald is one of their favorite things.

~~~~~~~~~~~~~~~~~~~~~~~~~~~~~

This compilation of some of Trump's most-admired items is based, of course, on "My Favorite Things," the Rodgers and Hammerstein song from *The Sound of Music*. (This is an update of an earlier version of this poem. For a refresher on Russia and Turkey in the last stanza, see the description accompanying "International Relations," the poem immediately preceding this one.)

The 2019 World Series

November 2, 2019

Politics is full of hate, but autumn baseball's always great!

———

Baseball was a fine distraction,
Without a right- or left-wing faction
(Except the game when Trump appeared
And many people booed and jeered).
Debates were over strikes and balls,
Not taxes, guns, or building walls.
Republicans and Democrats
Wore matching tees and baseball hats.
They skipped the news about impeachers
And had a blast in bars and bleachers.
Together they'd applaud and scream
To motivate their chosen team—
The Houston Astros or the Nats,
Two stellar squads with potent bats.
Now baseball's over till the spring,
And party warfare's back in swing.

The 2019 World Series culminated with the Washington Nationals defeating the Houston Astros in Game 7 on October 30. When Trump attend Game 5 at Nationals Park in D.C., the crowd booed him. Spectators held a sign behind home plate calling for Trump's impeachment. (This poem is an updated and expanded version of an April 2016 poem that appeared in *How it Happened: The 2016 Presidential Campaign in Jest and Verse.*)

The Next Phase

November 3, 2019

Impeachment reporting suffuses the news:
Did Trump, in his phone call, misuse and abuse
His power to garner political gain,
With foreign affairs as his private domain,
As if bribing Ukraine were a normal pursuit
Instead of a stunt by an unruly brute
To damage a probable rival's repute?

The House now—in public—will probe and play sleuth
To gather the facts and uncover the truth.

~~~~~~

"House Backs Impeachment!" was the thrust of nationwide headlines on October 31, 2019. In a near party-line split, the House of Representatives voted to formalize the impeachment inquiry into Trump, laying the groundwork for the public phase of the investigation, including televised hearings. During the prior five weeks, congressional investigators had been interviewing witnesses in private, with the substance of their testimony sometimes leaked to the press. The revelations from the closed-door hearings gave Democrats the confidence to take the impeachment inquiry to the next phase. In fact, on the same day that the House formalized the impeachment, the *Washington Post* reported that a top national security official, in a closed-door session, corroborated previous testimony that Trump had used his presidential power to withhold military aid to Ukraine, unless Ukraine investigated Joe Biden and his son.

Katie Hill: Throuple Trouble

November 5, 2019

She did *not* pay a porn star or grope on a plane,
But her judgment was wanting, with nothing to gain.
Campaigning for Congress entails lots of stress,
But better to stave off a personal mess,
'Cause when you're in public, affairs come to light,
And then you are in for a dastardly fight.

Transmitting lewd pics of one's ex without clothes
Is revenge porn—a crime, as her husband now knows.
Yes, *she* was a victim as well as a culprit;
Conservative shamers should get off their pulpit.

Men have gotten their way for innumerous years
With minimal harm to their public careers.
But the House passed new rules in the wake of MeToo—
What's good for the gander is good for "SheToo."

~~~~~~~~~~~~~~~~~~~~~~

Democrat Katie Hill, at 33, was elected to Congress in 2018 in a California district long under Republican control. Less than a year later, while she was going through a divorce, a right-wing website reported that she had an affair with her (male) legislative director and that she and her husband had engaged in a long-term sexual relationship with a (female) campaign worker. Internet sites published sexually explicit photographs of Hill without her consent, and Hill claimed they were released by her estranged husband. The House Ethics Committee announced it would investigate the allegation of Hill's affair with the legislative director. If true, she would be in violation of a House ethics rule implemented in 2018 in light of the #MeToo movement. Shortly after the House announcement, Hill confirmed the relationship with the campaign worker, acknowledging that it was inappropriate because the woman was a subordinate. Hill, however, denied the affair with her legislative director, as did he. Even so, she resigned from Congress on November 3, 2019, stating that it was "the best thing for my constituents and our country." She claimed there was a "double standard" for men and women in public life, and also vowed to combat revenge porn.

Michael Bloomberg: Run or Run Away?

November 8, 2019

He's fervent on gun safety, firmly pro-choice—
His billions give Bloomberg an oversized voice.
The climate concerns him; so too public health—
He tries to do good with his staggering wealth.

But *really* now, *should* he be running for POTUS?
Perhaps he can be more pragmatic and notice
That Sanders and Warren are hitting a nerve—
Their fans believe billionaires no way deserve
To gobble up wealth without paying their share
While regular wage earners sink in despair.
And Bloomberg's support of New York's stop and frisk
Perhaps would put Democrats too much at risk.
For *New York Times* columnist Charles M. Blow
That stance by itself meant a definite NO.

So think it through clearly, Mike, please test it out—
Perhaps make a run if you're sure there's no doubt
That *you'll* gain approval from "stop and frisk" foes
And young people, liberals, everyday Joes,
And farmers and unions and Black people too—
But Mike, that's not something I think you can do!

~~~~~~~~~~~~~~~~~~~~

On November 7, 2019, Michael Bloomberg, the billionaire former mayor of New York City, announced that he would seek the 2020 Democratic nomination for president, even though he had stated in March that he wouldn't be running. By October 2019, he had begun to reconsider because Joe Biden was starting to struggle against the more left-wing Elizabeth Warren. Bloomberg, a moderate, was one of Warren's biggest critics from the Democratic side. Bloomberg's main goal, however, was to prevent the reelection of Trump. Politically, Bloomberg always followed his own path, supporting both liberal and conservative causes. For example, he supports gun-safety measures, abortion rights, public health initiatives, and policies to combat climate change. On the other hand, Bloomberg is more Wall Street-friendly than many Democrats. In addition, he advocated stop-and-frisk policing when he was mayor; that alone was enough for *New York Times* columnist Charles M. Blow to write a scathing column rejecting Bloomberg.

Two-Time Governor Deval Patrick

November 15, 2019

Is it too late for Patrick
To pull a deft hat trick
And hasten his pace
To enter the race?

The plusses for Patrick?
He's not geriatric.
He's skilled at oration.
He gets the vexation
That millions are feeling
And knows we need healing.

But he now works at Bain
(Which was Romney's domain),
So the left will complain
And make Patrick explain
His pro-business views
And *why* he would choose
To aid corporate giants
And *not* needy clients.

Yet he grew up in need
And worked hard to succeed.
So his backstory's good,
But does *that* mean he should
Throw his hat in the ring?
What new strengths does he bring
That his rivals are short of?
Can he gain the support of
The key states that Trump won,
And if not, then why run?
It's too *early* to know,

So why *not* let him show
If he *has* the right stuff
And is forceful enough
To break through the din
And possibly win.

Top Democrats had encouraged Deval Patrick, two-time governor of Massachu-setts, to join the presidential race, but he decided against it in December 2018, citing the "cruelty" of the process. Later, with doubts about the Democrats' abil-ity to defeat Trump, Patrick changed his mind and, on November 14, 2019, for-mally entered the race. In many ways, he was a good candidate: experienced, successful, and younger than the top contenders, with strong oratory skills. As a moderate Democratic, he would probably be able to attract a broader range of voters than the more leftist candidates. He also has a good backstory: raised by his mother in a Chicago housing project, he graduated from Harvard College and Harvard Law School. After serving two terms as governor of Massachusetts, he joined Bain Capital, the private equity firm co-founded by Mitt Romney. (As hockey fans and Merriam-Webster users know, a "hat trick" is "a series of three victories, successes, or related accomplishments." Patrick withdrew from the presidential race in February 2020; he did not pull a political hat trick.)

Honey Money vs. Hush Money

November 21, 2019

Ms. Klobuchar's exes are not feckless schmucks.
They gave her campaigns many thousands of bucks.
For Trump, though, the dough went the opposite way.
To *silence* his exes, the man had to pay!

~~~~~~~~~~~~~~~~~~~~

In the fifth Democratic presidential debate (November 20, 2019), Senator Amy Klobuchar (D-MN) mentioned that she raised $17,000 from ex-boyfriends in her first Senate race, adding that that group of donors was "not an expanding base." She raised the money by hauling out old address books and asking everyone she knew for contributions. She didn't note the contrast between *her* treatment of exes and Trump's, but it does suggest itself.

2020

2020 was a tumultuous and unprecedented twelve months that sometimes seemed twice as long. Overarching everything was the Covid-19 pandemic, which would eventually kill millions. To curb the spread of the disease, the country shut down: workplaces and schools closed, and people started social distancing, quarantining, washing their hands frequently, and wearing face masks. The pandemic came on the heels of the impeachment trial and acquittal of Donald Trump. In late May, a brutal act of violence stunned the nation: the death of an unarmed Black man, George Floyd, under the knee of a police officer. Floyd's death sparked worldwide protests against police brutality and racism. At a protest in Lafayette Square in Washington, D.C., federal law-enforcement officers cleared peaceful protesters with tear gas and rubber bullets, seemingly to allow Trump to pose for a photo with a Bible in front of a nearby church. 2020 was also a year of major changes in U.S. politics. Supreme Court Justice Ruth Bader Ginsburg died, and the Republicans rushed to replace her to solidify right-wing control of the Court, even with the presidential election around the corner. Joe Biden became the Democratic nominee for president and selected Senator Kamala Harris as his running mate, making her the first woman of color to appear on a major-party ticket for vice president. When Biden and Harris won the election, Trump launched his "stop the steal" campaign, falsely but blatantly claiming that the election was stolen. Despite all the tumult, a couple who could live anywhere chose the U.S.: Prince Harry and Meghan Markle quit the British royal family and split for California.

Escape

January 4, 2020

When news becomes too hard for me to face,
I read a book about another place.
I watch a film about another time.
I write a verse that doesn't have to rhyme.

I dream about a tropical escape.
I take a winter beach trip to the Cape.
I buy a finer quality of wine.
I browse—for things I'll never need—online.

I act as if I haven't got a care.
Reality's too harrowing to bear.
But sometime when I'm fully back on board,
Please fill me in on all that I've ignored.

~~~~~~~~~~~~~~~~~~~~~~~~~~~~~~~~~~~~~

The news was full of death, danger, and deceit in the first few days of 2020. Just a few hours into the new year, gun violence claimed lives across the country—in Cleveland, Houston, Philadelphia, St. Louis, and elsewhere. On January 3, a controversial drone strike ordered by Trump killed a powerful Iranian military commander near the Baghdad airport, and Iran vowed revenge. In Australia, out-of-control wildfires that began in 2019 continued to rage. Record-high temperatures, fierce winds, and severe drought threatened even greater devastation. The *New York Times* on January 3 reported that the Trump administration was withholding twenty emails between a White House aide and the official at the Office of Management and Budget responsible for releasing congressionally mandated military aid to Ukraine—more data at the core of Trump's impeachment. News buffs aborbed all this, and more, only four days into the year. No wonder some of them craved an escape. Little did they know that a pandemic was imminent.

A Royal Mess

January 12, 2020

In France, heads rolled; in Russia too,
Yet Britain's crown is "tried and true."
But could the Megxit quest undo
Traditions that have gone askew
And let the Windsor House come through
Refreshed, revamped, and born anew?

The queen should fully think it through,
And though she's likely to eschew
Extensive change that might unglue
The monarchy from British life,
She might be wise to curb the strife
By hearing out Prince Harry's wife.

~~~~~~~~~~~~~~~~~~~~~~~~~~~~~~~~~~~~~

In January 2020, Britain's Prince Harry, Duke of Sussex, and his wife, Meghan, Duchess of Sussex, announced that they would "step back" from their duties as members of the British royal family and "balance [their] time between the United Kingdom and North America." Royal-watchers turned to Queen Elizabeth to see how she would handle the matter, which quickly became known as "Megxit," a play on the portmanteau "Brexit." Opinions on Megxit were divided—was it an admirable act of democratically inspired self-definition, or an unwarranted subversion of the monarchy? Queen Elizabeth called a family meeting for January 13, the day after this poem, to discuss the situation. (Update: Although this poem recommended "hearing out" Meghan Markle, she and Prince Harry, nearly three years later, went overboard in recounting their romance and rehashing their grievances in a six-part Netflix series. Then, in January 2023, Harry's memoir, *Spare*, arrived, with TMI, including multiple mentions of his penis, often in British slang, and silly anecdotes about spats between Kate Middleton and Meghan. More significantly, the book lambasted the intrusive British press and revealed the machinations and vanity of the monarchy, making Harry and Meghan's exit understandable.)

Sign-Stealing: Morality Plays

January 21, 2020

Spot a signal, be a spy.
Do it with your naked eye!
That's accepted in the game,
But *watch out* if you do the same
With modern gear and high-tech tools
'Cause that would violate the rules.
The punishment would be severe,
Perhaps destroying your career.
Will M.L.B. deploy new tech
To keep the theft of signs in check?

~~~~~~~~~~~~~~~~~~~~~~~~~~~~~~~~~

On January 13, 2020, Major League Baseball (M.L.B.) announced that the Houston Astros, who won the 2017 World Series, had stolen pitchers' signs illegally throughout the 2017 season and post-season. M.L.B. fired the team's general manager and manager, fined the team five million dollars (the maximum allowed), and deprived it of several top draft picks. Although the Astros clearly cheated under M.L.B. rules and were rightfully punished, some sports ethicists and writers pondered the sometimes-blurry line between legitimate trickery—long part of baseball—and cheating. Sign-stealing with the naked eye, on the field, is allowed. It is acceptable for a runner on second base to observe a catcher's signal (a public act) and convey it to the batter. The Astros, however, deployed a camera feed from center field, and then, through a "relay" that included a television monitor and banging on a trash can, the information was conveyed to the batter. (Fast-forward two years: for the 2022 season, M.L.B. introduced PitchCom, a wireless communication device that allows the catcher to communicate with the pitcher without using visible signs.)

Impeachment Trial and Acquittal of Donald Trump
January 16–February 5, 2020

Even though the impeachment trial and acquittal of Trump were momentous events in American history, they didn't inspire a poem for this collection.

The charges against Trump were strong: (1) *abuse of power* for soliciting foreign interference in the 2020 U.S. presidential election, i.e., for withholding security aid to pressure Ukraine's president to announce an investigation into Trump's likely rival in the election, and (2) *obstruction of Congress* for ordering his administration to ignore the House's subpoenas and requests during the impeachment investigation.

The result was an acquittal on both charges. The vote was along party lines (with the two Independent senators voting with the Democrats to convict), with one exception: Republican Senator Mitt Romney of Utah voted to convict Trump on the first count.

Election Rant

February 6, 2020

Hey, Iowans, you'd better scrap
That slapped-together caucus app,
And while you're trying things anew,
Please ditch the caucus concept too.
And why is *Iowa* the place
That's first in line for every race?
I'm also totally perplexed
On why New Hampshire's always next.
And why oh why do we denote
A *Tuesday* as the day to vote?
And why on earth must we succumb
Like clockwork, each quadrennium,
To people called "electors" who
We'll never know and never knew?
Democracy in our great land
Is often hard to understand.

~~~~~~~~~~~~~~~~~~~~~~

The Iowa caucuses are a convoluted process through which Iowans, both Democrats and Republicans, select the delegates for their national party conventions. Instead of casting votes in a primary, Iowans convene in small groups at various venues, including libraries, schools, and private homes, and discuss the candidates and the issues. Then they cluster into smaller groups to display their endorsement of a specific candidate. Uncommitted voters are wooed by the various factions. Many people outside Iowa don't understand the caucus procedure, even after they've read (or written) multiple explanations of it, including this one.

The Iowa caucus selects about 1.2% of the delegates to the Democratic convention, but, as the first major contest in a presidential primary season, it is covered obsessively. The media's interpretation of it tends to have a large—and disproportionate—effect on the campaign. In 2020, this process was more complicated than usual because of a poorly designed phone app that threw the Iowa Democratic caucus into chaos and resulted in a week's delay in reporting the result. After Iowa, all eyes turn to New Hampshire, where the total population, in 2019, was 1.36 million—less than, for example, the population of San Diego—and, like Iowa, overwhelmingly white.

Many established democracies designate election day as a national holiday or hold elections on a weekend. Others allow in-person voting over a multi-day or multi-week period. The U.S., however, clings to Tuesday (although Americans can vote early by mail or ballot drop box). People in other countries are often surprised that the U.S. presidency is not determined by popular vote, but by the preponderance of votes of "electors" in the Electoral College. All these factors contribute to an electoral system thought by many to be dysfunctional (even apart from issues involving voting rights and voter suppression).

Despotic Design
February 10, 2020

Mandatory architecture, style by the State,
Dictator-decreed design, unopen for debate.
Mussolini, Hitler, helped along by Albert Speer,
Favored symmetry and columns—chilly, white, austere.
Donald Trump built shiny towers, shrieking out his name,
Even so there's worry that his White House will proclaim,
In spite of his affection for flamboyant gold and gilt,
That future public architecture *must* be planned and built
With fusty fascist columns, formulaic to the core,
Making our environment an uninspired bore.

〜〜〜〜〜〜〜〜〜〜〜

A draft executive order, called "Making Federal Buildings Beautiful Again," decreed that "classical" would be the "preferred and default style" for many federal buildings. Architects and urban planners opposed the order, believing it would curtail innovation. Despots, of course, sometimes dictate the style of public buildings. Mussolini and Hitler (and Hitler's architect, Albert Speer) did, turning to "grand classicism" to glorify their regimes.

There are beautiful classical buildings; there are banal classical buildings. There are impressive modern buildings; there are ugly ones, too. The same goes for other styles. But the point is that the government should no more mandate a style of architecture than it should dictate styles in painting or fiction. In the draft executive order, any project seeking exemption from the classical decree would have to get approval from a presidential "re-beautification" committee. That sounds like something out of George Orwell, if not the Soviet Union. (In December 2020, after the date of this poem, Trump signed the executive order, renamed "Promoting Beautiful Federal Civic Architecture," but Biden revoked it in February 2021.)

Abide in Biden!

March 4, 2020

Hiding in the undecided mind,
Biden staged a comeback from behind.
Bernie's engine lost a little steam.
Warren's chances faded to a dream.
Pete and Amy stopped their silly spat,
Bowing out and helping Joe combat
The surging leftist faction that they fear
Will catalyze a win for Trump this year.
And Bloomberg's words were graceful in goodbye.
For him, a billion dollars isn't high.
His hefty wallet now will go to Biden
In hopes that Joe's new dominance will widen.
They all agree on one objective, though:
To save our nation, Donald Trump must go!

~~~~~~

Biden performed poorly in the first two presidential nominating contests: he came in fourth in Iowa and fifth in New Hampshire, not even receiving delegates in the latter. On March 3, 2020—Super Tuesday—fourteen states held their presidential primaries, with 34% of the total Democratic delegates at stake. Representative James Clyburn (D-SC) had endorsed Joe Biden in South Carolina's primary three days earlier, helping Biden win there and giving his moribund campaign much-needed momentum. When Biden won Alabama, Arkansas, Maine, Massachusetts, Minnesota, North Carolina, Oklahoma, Tennessee, Texas, and Virginia on Super Tuesday, he emerged as the clear leader. Bernie Sanders won California; Elizabeth Warren (and Tulsi Gabbard) failed to win any state. Michael Bloomberg, having spent about a billion dollars of his own money on his short-lived campaign, managed to win only American Samoa and bowed out. Senator Amy Klobuchar (D-MN) and former South Bend, Indiana, Mayor Pete Buttigieg, who all but came to blows in a debate on February 20, put aside their differences, and their midwestern centrist rivalry, to support Biden.

Plagued

March 13, 2020

Wash your hands and count to twenty!
Toilet paper—we bought plenty!
Eyes may itch, but we don't touch.
Clorox wipes cost twice as much.
Quarantines have been imposed.
Colleges and schools have closed.
Concerts, plays, and sports have stopped.
Stocks around the globe have dropped.
Supermarket shelves are bare.
Shoppers buy long-lasting fare.
Pantries now are full of pasta.
Daily life is out of Kafka.

~~~~~~~~~~~~~~~~~~~~~~~~~~~~~~~~

In March 2020, the U.S. started to face the grim—and surreal—experience of Covid-19 and lockdown. This led to barren supermarket shelves as shoppers grabbed (and hoarded) such fundamentals as toilet paper, paper towels, and sanitizing wipes, and stocked up on beans, pasta, and other foods with long shelf lives. At the outset of the pandemic, people were afraid they could contract Covid-19 from surfaces. Experts advised everyone to wash their hands for twenty seconds after touching things outside their homes and to avoid touching their faces, especially the eyes, nose, and mouth. (Experts were not yet recommending masks.) Many people were afraid to handle their incoming mail and packages. Colleges and other schools started to close. On March 11, the N.B.A. suspended its games until further notice because a player tested positive for Covid-19, and on March 12, M.L.B. announced that it was delaying its season. An essay in the *New York Times* suggested writing poems because Broadway was closed, and some people complied.

Poetic Justice
March 19, 2020

Joe promised he'd opt for a woman as veep,
And this is a vow I am sure he will keep.
It means he will *not* go with Cory or Pete,
But still, he'll find someone to help him unseat
Our spiteful and hollow commander in chief
And bring to our nation rebirth and relief.
Though Harris or Abrams would each fit the bill,
I think he should opt for . . . Anita Hill!

~~~~~~~~~~~~~~~~~~~~~~~~~

Joe Biden, who had promised to pick a woman as his running mate, was under pressure to select a woman of color. Among the choices were Senator Kamala Harris (D-CA) and voting rights activist Stacey Abrams. Many voters remembered Biden's treatment of Anita Hill, the African American law professor who accused Clarence Thomas of sexual harassment in his 1991 Supreme Court nomination hearings. Biden, then chairman of the Senate Judiciary Committee, gave Hill short shrift and, in a "compromise" with Senate Republicans, failed to call other women whose testimony could have confirmed Hill's allegations. (The "recommendation" in this poem isn't serious; it is based on a wry comment, a joke, made by two different people when Biden was contemplating his vice-presidential pick.)

Viral Insomnia

March 20, 2020

My head's on my pillow; I'm breathing through sobs.
I worry for everyone losing their jobs.

My foot's on the headboard; I'm still wide awake.
I'm scared that vaccines will take too long to make.

It's 3, I'm alert, sleep won't come, I just know it.
I fear we're not doing the right things to slow it.

I worry for people much older than I. . . .
Will triage and scarcity force them to die?

I worry for Michigan, Italy, Spain,
As death tolls go up and their resources drain.

I took a Lunesta and started to snooze
But dreamt I was trapped on an overseas cruise.

At dawn I awakened, exhausted as hell,
And vowed that there's one thing on which I won't dwell—

I'll follow the guidelines, stay in, wash my hands,
But ration the news to occasional scans.

~~~~~~~~~~~~~~~~~~~~~~

Early in the pandemic, the "novel coronavirus" (as it was called then) was an alarming mystery. Could you catch Covid-19 by touching a surface that had the virus on it? In case you could, many of us washed or disinfected the food packages we brought home from the supermarket, or left them in a separate room for a couple of days. Similarly, we disinfected our mail and delivery parcels or let them sit for forty-eight hours. Many people were losing their jobs, especially in the leisure and hospitality sectors. On March 19, Italy overtook China as the country with the most reported deaths from Covid-19. Michigan and Spain were other early hotspots. At least twenty-five cruise ships had Covid-19 outbreaks; the virus spread easily in close quarters. Vaccines were not yet available, and no one outside specialized scientific communities could imagine that a vaccine would be developed relatively quickly. The news was full of articles about the 1918 flu pandemic, which resulted in about fifty million deaths worldwide (according to some estimates), with about six hundred and seventy-five thousand in the United States. The multiple unknowns—and the fear of catching the virus—triggered anxiety and fear. There was ample cause to lose sleep.

Listless

March 30, 2020

I wear nightgowns from morning to night.
I am quarantined, well out of sight.

Food is low; I am now in a crunch,
So it's pasta for breakfast and lunch.

I still bathe but I grudgingly groom,
And wear lipstick now only for Zoom.

My hair is outgrowing its style.
I wash it just once in a while.

The mending that I'd undertaken
Now sits in a corner, forsaken.

The books I've been meaning to read
Will never get read, I concede.

Decluttering, purging—such tedious tasks.
I'll skip them for now, but I'll make room for masks.

My friends say "do yoga online!"
Instead I lie prone and drink wine.

"Do tap or ballet from your phone!"
Instead I drink wine and lie prone.

"Go walk, breathe fresh air, see the sky!"
Instead I stay cloistered and cry.

I'm frozen in place; it's disturbing, foreboding,
While outside my haven the country's imploding.

Some people became productive with the extra time they gained during the Covid lockdown—reorganizing their bookshelves, scanning old photos, decluttering closets, reading books they had always meant to read, continuing their workouts through phone apps, and sewing and distributing cloth masks. Others exemplified a paradox of the lockdown: the more free time one had, the more lethargic and unproductive one became. Part of this may have been due to the ever-dispiriting news, including Trump's failure to deal with the pandemic responsibly. On March 24, 2020, he said he wanted the country "opened up and raring to go" by Easter, a little more than two weeks away, even though the number of Covid-19 cases continued to rise, hospitals faced a shortage of medical supplies, and health experts warned of a worsening crisis. Many people were becoming depressed. Multiple businesses started to fail, but liquor stores were thriving and psychologists couldn't keep up with demand.

Wish

April 13, 2020

The weeks go by, the fourth, the fifth,
And normalcy's become a myth.
I want to hug, I want to hold,
I want this deadly scourge controlled.
I want to walk amidst a crowd.
I want to lift this morbid shroud.
I sit, sequestered in my home,
And yearn to mingle, travel, roam.
My energy is out of whack—
I want my normal problems back.

~~~~~~

For many, a month of pandemic lockdown seemed like years. The jarring, un-settling new reality—distress, anxiety, social isolation, sickness, loss, grief—eclipsed the ordinary problems of day-to-day life. (This poem started out as lyrics based on Leonard Cohen's "Hallelujah.")

Knees

May 31, 2020

A brute policeman used his knee,
A nine-minute atrocity.
Then crowds reacted, shocked and fraught.
At last a murder charge was brought.

A football player took a knee,
A quiet act of dignity,
But outrage flared—he lost his job,
Accosted by a Twitter mob.

Will Minnesota's tragedy
Make those incensed by Colin see
The impetus behind his knee
Before the next catastrophe?

We pray another one won't happen,
But plainly there's a massive gap in
The white and Black reality,
So follow Colin: take a knee.

~~~~~~

George Floyd, a Black former security guard, was detained by police on May 25, 2020, in Minneapolis after a store clerk suspected him of paying with a counterfeit twenty-dollar bill. One officer kept Floyd pinned to the ground—facedown and handcuffed—by pressing a knee on his neck for about nine minutes. Floyd said "I can't breathe" multiple times and died under the officer's knee.

Quarterback Colin Kaepernick famously took a knee, instead of standing, for the national anthem at various San Francisco 49ers football games in 2016 to protest racism and police mistreatment of minorities. After he became a free agent in March 2017, he was unable to find a position in the N.F.L., despite good stats. He later filed a grievance against the N.F.L. and reached a settlement.

Unholy

June 3, 2020

A peaceful crowd with medics, priests,
Was treated like unruly beasts
So Trump could stage a photo op,
A Bible, upside down, the prop.
Ivanka wore a pricey purse,
Which made the scene seem even worse.
The despot's daughter, blithely strolling,
Observed the armed police patrolling.
Their rubber bullets, smoke, and gas
Had cleared the crowd so Trump could pass.
And standing near was William Barr
(Who thinks that Trump should be a czar).
Instead of words or thoughts on race,
We saw a tyrant-like disgrace.

~~~~~~~~~~~~~~~~~~~~~~~~~~~~~~~

On June 1, 2020, less than a week after George Floyd was killed, Donald Trump gave a speech in the White House Rose Garden. Although he expressed sympathy for the families of Black people killed by police, he spent more time denouncing the people *protesting* police brutality. He threatened to send the U.S. military to cities that did not rein in protesters.

Trump then walked across Lafayette Square, a park outside the White House, to historic St. John's Church. The U.S. Park Police, the D.C. National Guard, the D.C. Police, and other law-enforcement officers, some in riot gear, had just forcibly dispersed—with tear gas, smoke canisters, and rubber bullets—a peaceful crowd of protesters in the square, including clergy and volunteers offering snacks and water. Several Trump administration officials accompanied the president, including Attorney General William Barr, an advocate of expansive presidential power (at least when the president is a Republican). Also on the scene was Trump's daughter Ivanka, elegant and oblivious as she carried a $1,540 designer handbag. Inside it was a Bible, which she handed to her father.

Once in front of the church, Trump wordlessly brandished the Bible, upside down. It was a gesture of comic-opera arrogance and quickly drew condemnation from military and religious figures across the country. Calling the aggressive expulsion of protesters "an abuse of executive authority," James Mattis, Trump's first secretary of defense, wrote, "Never did I dream that troops . . . would be ordered under any circumstance to violate the Constitutional rights of their fellow citizens." Reverend James Martin, a well-known Jesuit priest and author, said, "Using the Bible as a prop while talking about sending in the military . . . is pretty much the opposite of all Jesus stood for." Prominent Republicans also criticized Trump. For example, Senator Ben Sasse (R-NE) said, "[T]here is a . . . Constitutional . . . right to protest, and I'm against clearing out a peaceful protest for a photo op that treats the Word of God as a political prop." General Mark Milley, then chairman of the Joint Chiefs of Staff, had walked across Lafayette Square with Trump, but soon apologized, saying he was wrong to be there. (About a year later, an investigation led by a Trump appointee found that the U.S. Park Police had cleared the protesters so that a contractor could install scale-proof fencing, not to let Trump walk through the square for a photo op. Some journalists and political analysts didn't trust the report, for a variety of reasons. For example, the inquiry focused on the Park Police and not the actions of officers from other law-enforcement agencies in Lafayette Square that day, including the D.C. Police, the Bureau of Prisons, and the Secret Service.)

Cronyism Spells Doom

June 20, 2020

When ancient Rome was smoldering,
    Nero played his fiddle.
When America was blundering,
    Donald won acquittal.

And since then checks on power
    are becoming more ephemeral,
With firings for no reason
    of some fine inspectors general.

Now every day another step toward despotism comes.
The prosecutor scrutinizing actions by Trump chums
Appears to have been sacked, although we're not yet sure by whom,
But whether Trump or Barr, this new dismissal signals doom,
Yes, doom for our democracy, the Founders' noble cause,
If sycophants and cronies thwart a government of laws.

~~~~~~~~~~~~~~~~~~~~~~~~~~~~~~

In June 2020, Trump fired Geoffrey Berman, a Republican, Trump donor, and head of the high-profile U.S. Attorney's Office for the Southern District of New York. (After a snafu in which Berman, at first, said he wasn't leaving, Trump tried to distance himself from the situation, saying it was Attorney General William Barr's responsibility.) Berman's office had prosecuted Michael Cohen, Trump's former personal attorney, and had also indicted two associates of Rudy Giuliani, Trump's attorney at the time, for complex campaign-finance shenanigans. Investigations into Giuliani's dealings with the two were still underway. Berman was also handling a criminal case against a state-owned Turkish bank and its officers, but the president of Turkey, Recep Erdogan, was pressuring Trump to halt it, and Trump was eager to accommodate Erdogan.

    Many observers blasted the firing of Berman as corrupt and unethical, undermining the rule of law and the independence of the U.S. Attorney's Office. It seemed that Trump was interfering in criminal investigations he disliked.

The firing of Berman was similar to Trump's ousters of inspectors general—independent federal watchdogs—whose investigations he found threatening. In the spring of 2020, Trump removed five inspectors general in a span of six weeks. For example, he fired Glenn Fine—who had a reputation for integrity in both Democratic and Republican administrations—as the watchdog overseeing the Covid relief effort, after Fine had spent just a week in the role, and replaced him with a loyalist (hence the "fine inspectors general" line in the poem).

Stop This Posthaste!

August 3, 2020

Neither snow nor rain nor Trump nor hail
Will thwart our honest votes by mail!

———

As history taught us in childhood,
America's mail was a force for good,
Bringing together our growing nation—
Even small towns had a postal station.

Though we complain it gets lost or is slow,
Most of the time we are happy to know
A card from the East will arrive in the West
In just a few days if correctly addressed.

But now a Trump donor is post office head,
And voting rights advocates shudder in dread.
This crony is changing procedures in ways
That clog up the system and lead to delays.

With Covid it's crucial that ballots by mail
Be processed with speed and dispatched without fail.
A backlog of ballots arriving too late
Will certainly *not* make America great.
Not "again" and not ever; it's just one more fraud
That Trump and his cronies concoct and applaud.

~~~~~~~~~~~~~~~

Trump (correctly) feared that the easier it was for people to vote, the worse his chances for re-election. Many believed that was why he named Louis DeJoy, a major Republican donor, as postmaster general. Because of the Covid pandemic, the U.S. postal system was more important than ever to ensure that citizens could vote by mail. DeJoy promptly announced plans to cut employee overtime and reduce the number of postal-sorting machines, among other changes, ostensibly as cost-saving measures. Many were outraged, contending that these actions were instead part of a political effort to undermine absentee voting. (Two weeks after the date of this poem, amid the furor that followed DeJoy's announcement, he issued a statement: "To avoid even the appearance of any impact on election mail, I am suspending these initiatives until after the election is concluded.")

Only A Game
August 28, 2020

It was *Only A Game*,
And today it's a shame
That a long-running show
Had nowhere to go
Except off the air.

Its listeners care.
It went well beyond sports
With its quirky reports.

A podcast may save it
For people who crave it.
But it *won't* be the same,
And just *what* is to blame?
A Covid-caused layoff
And funding that's *way* off.

Though its money was shrinking,
This was still short-term thinking.

~~~~~~~~~~~~~~~~~~~~~~~~~~~~~~~~~~~~~~

In the pandemic-damaged economy, institutions that depended on donations, such as National Public Radio (NPR) stations, suffered significant reductions in revenue. As a result, WBUR, an NPR station in Boston, announced it would reduce staff and halt production of *Only A Game*, NPR's only sports program. It had run since 1993 on more than 260 NPR stations, featuring compelling stories about a wide range of sports, from the mainstream to the offbeat. Its termination was a blow to informed, intelligent broadcast journalism.

Mitch McConnell's Soliloquy

September 19, 2020

"Consistency's for chumps and fools!
I like to make up specious rules
That favor me no matter what.
I want to get a right-wing glut
To clinch the Court for years to come.
I won't give Democrats a crumb.
What? Pause a day to mourn for Ruth?
For once I'll tell the bald-faced truth:
I guiltlessly don't give a hoot.
Our need for speed is absolute!
No time to spare! No time to pause,
When voting rights and healthcare laws
Are on the books and must be crushed!
I'll get this brand-new justice rushed!
That Merrick Garland, *who* is *he*?
A sign of my hypocrisy?
It's diff'rent *this* time, I can crow:
We've found a way to make it so,
By splitting hairs creatively
To steamroll legislatively.
But Susan, Lisa, Mitt, and others
Might quash my chance to get my druthers."

~~~~~~

Supreme Court Justice Ruth Bader Ginsburg died on September 18, 2020. Less than two hours after news of her death broke, Senator Majority Leader Mitch McConnell (R-KY) vowed that Trump's nominee to replace her would get a vote on the Senate floor as soon as possible, the 2016 "Merrick Garland precedent" be damned. The hypocrisy was stunning: McConnell had refused to give Merrick Garland a hearing when President Obama nominated him in March 2016 to replace Justice Antonin Scalia, who died on February 13, 2016. After Scalia's death was announced, McConnell proclaimed it would be inappropriate to hold a Senate vote on a new Supreme Court justice because it was an election year, with election day nine months away. Now here was McConnell hurrying to confirm a new justice with an election just six *weeks* away, with early voting already underway in some states. McConnell and other Republican senators offered a questionable explanation of why this time was different: the Garland nomination occurred when the president and the Senate majority were of different political parties, whereas this time, they were of the same party. Democrats hoped that Republican moderates Susan Collins (ME), Lisa Murkowski (AK), and Mitt Romney (UT) would vote against holding hearings right away on Justice Ginsburg's replacement. In the end, the hearings were held, and no Democrats and all Republicans, except Collins, voted in favor of Trump's nominee, Amy Coney Barrett. She took her oath of office on October 27, a week before the presidential election.

Don't Bring a PowerPoint Show to a Gunfight!
September 22, 2020

When G.O.P. strategists plot and go low,
The Democrats work on a PowerPoint show
On a policy program, their "weapon" of choice,
And the smirking Republicans laugh and rejoice.

The Democrats cater to minds and to reason.
The G.O.P. mocks all their fancy degrees in
The law, public policy, foreign affairs,
Aware that their voters think "who the hell cares"
And vote not on fact but emotion and gut,
With high-minded Democrats stuck in their rut.

～～～～～～～～～～～～～～

At the 2016 Democratic Convention, Michelle Obama won thunderous applause when she said, regarding Republicans, "When they go low, we go high." What she neglected to add was, "When they go low and we go high, they often win." Republicans, for decades, have appealed to racism, anti-communist (or anti-socialist) paranoia, fear of crime, anti-immigrant views, and religious zeal to win votes, while Democrats have insisted on presenting programs and plans, objective facts, and high-minded calls for fairness. In addition, Republicans excel at crafting short, clever phrases that resonate with many voters. The point is *not* for Democrats to appeal to the same kinds of prejudices and fears that Republicans do. Instead, Democrats would be wise to cut back on presenting the details of their policy points and instead focus on the *benefits* they offer to voters—the *outcome* of their policies—with short, well-honed phrases that appeal to the gut and the heart.

Donald Ducks Responsibility

September 24, 2020

Did Putin pay bounties for killing our troops,
Believing that Donald's the biggest of dupes,
Persuaded that Donald would *not* call him out,
And smug in his judgment that Russia has clout?

He dominates Donald with skill and command,
And Donald won't care if democracy's damned.

Republican schemers employ tricky ruses,
But Russia outfoxes them all; it abuses
The internet, Facebook, electoral files,
And Trump always welcomes its tricks and its wiles.
He *won't* anger Russia, 'cause *if* he does, *then*
They won't interfere in his favor again!

This Russian seduction without repercussion
May very well lead to our country's destruction.

~~~~~~~~~~~~~~~~~~~~~~~~~~~

In the months leading up to the 2020 U.S. presidential election, Russia was constantly in the news. First came the bombshell allegation that Russian President Vladimir Putin had paid cash bounties to Taliban militants for killing U.S. troops in Afghanistan. Trump did not raise the issue when he last spoke to Putin, as critics said he should have, but it turned out (as the Biden White House announced in April 2021) that U.S. intelligence officials were not convinced the reports were credible. Then, in early September, excerpts from Nixon-toppler Bob Woodward's new book, *Rage*, revealed that Trump's former director of national intelligence, Dan Coats, had deep suspicions that Putin "had something" on Trump, even though there was no intelligence proof. Coats "could see no other explanation" for the president's fawning behavior toward Putin. Meanwhile, a secret C.I.A. assessment, revealed by the *Washington Post* on September 22, 2020, concluded that "Vladimir Putin and the most senior Russian officials" were "probably directing influence operations" to interfere in the 2020 presidential election by denigrating Joe Biden, boosting Donald Trump, and "fueling public discord" in the U.S.

The Unprecedented, Unpresidential Debate
(In Three Short Acts)
September 30, 2020

Debate Prep

I poured a glass of cabernet
And figured I would be okay,
But just in case, I bought a quart
Of ice cream and a Linzer torte
And vodka and tomato juice
And brownies and a mocha mousse.

The Debate

I turned on CNN and watched
As Wallace, very early, botched
His chance to run a smooth debate.
We saw him flinch and abdicate
His role to Donald's lies and drivel,
But Biden's words and tone were civil,
Well suited for a U.S. leader,
Unlike that racist bottom feeder.

I threw my wine in Donald's face
And yelled, "You odious disgrace!"
My far-off neighbors heard me shriek,
"Oh, shut your mouth and let Joe speak!"
I lobbed my brownies at the screen,
"You're callous, nasty, foul, and mean!"
I mashed my mousse in Donald's hair
And eyed him with a scornful glare.
My wine glass broke on Donald's head,
And now my poor TV was dead.

Aftermath

I missed the rest of that debate
And tried my best to self-sedate
With vodka, music, herbal tea,
A book of light-verse poetry. . . .
I drifted off and dreamt that we
Recaptured grace and decency.

~~~~~~

The first Trump-Biden debate went down in history as the most appalling, out-of-control, and farcical presidential debate since the invention of television. Trump bullied, sneered, harangued, and interrupted constantly. He also talked over the hapless, overmatched moderator, Chris Wallace of Fox News. Trump even gave a positive shout-out to the Proud Boys, a violent, neo-fascist hate group. Most commentators thought Trump alienated moderates and independents with his unalloyed belligerence, which at one point inspired Biden to deliver the quote of the evening: "Shut up, man!" The debate was widely panned: Jake Tapper of CNN called it "a hot mess, inside a dumpster fire, inside a train wreck," and his colleague Dana Bash called it a "sh*t show." The *Washington Post's* editorial board said the debate demonstrated that "Trump has nothing but contempt for the values and norms that are essential to democracy: among them, truth, civility and respectful disagreement."

Covidiocy: Trump Gets Covid-19

October 4, 2020

Some thought it was a hoax—that's no surprise—
The White House always fabricates and lies.
It soon was very clear that it was true,
The trip to Walter Reed a telltale clue.

He knew his close aide Hicks had caught the bug
But still he went to mingle, talk, and hug
With donors at his swank New Jersey club.
But why expose them all? Well, there's the rub.

Did he really think that wearing masks was weak?
Or that Covid only bothered with the meek?
Did he think the virus, on its own, would wane
When he knew about the death of Herman Cain
From attending Tulsa's maskless, reckless rally
And increasing our alarming death-rate tally?

Yes, some believe it's karma—is that cruel?
But *this* is no surprise—he was a fool
For disregarding truth and expertise,
Politicizing healthcare and disease,
Ignoring guidance from the C.D.C.,
Embracing fringe hypotheses with glee.

We'll see if Trump recovers. If he does,
Will his behavior stay the way it was?

〜〜〜〜〜〜〜〜〜〜〜〜〜〜〜

On October 2, 2020, Trump announced that he and his wife had tested positive for Covid-19. Later that day, he was hospitalized at the Walter Reed medical center, where he was treated with remdesivir and monoclonal antibodies.

Trump may have contracted the virus from Hope Hicks, one of his close advisors. White House officials knew that she had tested positive for it and that the president had traveled with her on Air Force One and a helicopter earlier in the week. Aware that he had been exposed to the virus, Trump nonetheless attended a fundraiser on October 1 at his New Jersey golf club, where, unmasked and socializing, he might have infected dozens of others. Donors who attended the event were "freaking out," according to a source cited by cnbc.com (October 2, 2020). (The answer to the question in the last stanza: having Covid did *not* change Trump's irresponsible behavior and politicization of the pandemic.)

Pence vs. Harris

October 8, 2020

I watched with high anxiety
As Pence's crafty piety
Began to cover and disguise
His speciousness and blatant lies.

I watched with rising agitation
As Pence attempted domination,
Always going on too long,
Thinking that's what makes him strong.

I watched with worry on my face
As Harris spoke with force and grace
And held her own with dodgy Pence.
I loosened up, no longer tense.

I watched her sound analysis
Of Donald's Covid callousness.
She showed that she's well-paired with Biden
I hope she helps his lead to widen.

~~~~~~~~~~

The debate between Vice President Mike Pence and Democratic vice-presidential candidate Kamala Harris was, compared to the presidential debate the previous week, muted and low-key. Pence was smooth and glib, as befits a former radio-show host. Some Democrats were worried about Harris's performance because of Pence's on-air experience, but she held her own and was her usual witty, poised self. Neither side particularly drew blood, and no clear winner emerged—but that outcome was thought to favor the Democrats and Joe Biden, who continued to lead in the polls. In contrast to the agony of watching the first Biden-Trump debate, the most unpleasant aspect of this one was the frustration of witnessing Pence's various evasions and lies.

Election Angst

November 1, 2020

When politics becomes too hard to face,
I fantasize about a better place.
I buy a seven-liter jug of wine.
I lose myself in puzzle games online.
I Zoom with friends I'd rather see for real
And hide from them the way I truly feel.
I never tell them Zoloft is my crutch.
A triple dosage now is not too much.

But *so* what if I've gone a little nuts—
It's easy when you hate that scoundrel's guts.
He daily flouts our democratic norms,
And now our country sorely needs reforms,
With tyranny a step or two away
And ruthless Mitch McConnell holding sway
While civil-service job protections fray
And Covid cases fail to go away.

Each day we now confront a new "new low"
And wonder how much lower things can go.
And so, to cope, I've stopped consuming news,
Yes, even shows that validate my views.
Instead I watch old films with Fred Astaire
And dance along without a thought or care.
I read escapist books to tame my mind.
I play relaxing music to unwind.
I like it when I'm calm and unaware—
There's only so much anguish I can bear.
But sometime when I'm fully back on board,
You'll fill me in on all that I've ignored,
And while you're at it, kindly make a note
To text me so I won't forget to vote!

For many, the days preceding the 2020 presidential election on November 3 were awash in uncontainable anxiety and an unending seesaw of cautious optimism and prudent pessimism. The months leading to the election had been draining enough, with the unceasing Covid-19 pandemic, the accompanying economic downturn, Trump's inability to manage the pandemic, and the murder of George Floyd. Mitch McConnell had just maneuvered to get a right-wing justice onto the U.S. Supreme Court, Amy Coney Barrett, who took her judicial oath just a week before the election. The prior week, Trump had signed an executive order that weakened civil-service job protections, making federal employees easier to fire—not only politicizing the civil service, but also undermining longstanding laws aimed at preventing corruption and cronyism in the federal government. With one outrageous occurrence after another, many people were exasperated and depleted. Indeed, ever since Trump took office, the media had delivered an oppressive, exhausting marathon of disgraceful norm-breaking, cronyism, incompetence, and damage to international alliances. Hence this updated, revised, and expanded version of an earlier poem, "Escape," from January 4, 2020.

Election Tally
November 5, 2020 (1:30 a.m.)

Waiting, hoping
Barely coping

Adding, counting
Tension mounting

———————

Glued to news
Please don't lose

Doing math
Find a path

Change of state?
Still we wait . . .

~~~~~~

November 3—the day of the presidential election—ended without a conclusive winner. Some states were too close to call, and millions of votes were still being counted in key battleground states, including Georgia, Michigan, Nevada, North Carolina, Pennsylvania, and Wisconsin. After midnight, Biden advised his supporters to be patient while the votes were tallied, noting that he thought he was "on track" to win. About two hours later, Trump falsely proclaimed victory and called for the counting to stop. At 11:20 p.m. on election day, Fox News had projected that Biden would win Arizona, angering the Trump campaign. The Associated Press (AP) made the same projection close to 3 a.m. on Wednesday, but other major news organizations, including ABC, CBS, NBC, and CNN, still considered Arizona too close to call. By Wednesday evening, November 4, AP reported that Biden had won Michigan and Wisconsin, making him just six Electoral College votes away from victory. Georgia, Nevada, North Carolina, and Pennsylvania remained uncalled at 1:30 a.m. on November 5, when this poem emerged. Many people found it hard to cope with their anxiety and the uncertainty as the counting continued. Even so, Biden's less neurotic supporters were cautiously optimistic as the Electoral College math revealed pathways to victory.

Biden, Victor | Trump, Contradictor
(or Biden's Win | Trump's Spin)

November 7–17, 2020

A scream of relief!
I unclenched my teeth
And danced in the streets.
But then came the tweets
Denying the loss
And wanting to toss
The voting result
To please his damn cult
And save his thin skin
From Biden's clear win.

The G.O.P.'s shameless,
Supporting his brainless
Amoral persistence
And baseless insistence
That he was elected
Instead of rejected.

And Trump, your fixation
Is harming our nation.
You need to concede!
You cannot impede
A normal transition.
I don't seek contrition,
But get the hell out!
You lost without doubt.
Please let us have faith
That democracy's safe.

The Associated Press, Fox News, and other major news organizations called the election for Biden on November 7, 2020. Trump, a constant liar, unleashed what came to be known as the "Big Lie": his claim that *he* won the election and that it was "stolen" from him. The *Washington Post* calculated and documented that Trump told about 30,000 lies during his term. His followers believed those lies and found it easy to believe this one, too. What was more surprising was the degree to which Republican party officials, including members of Congress, professed (or pretended) to believe it—or, at least, evaded stating outright that Biden had won. (Little did we know that greater tumult was yet to come, on January 6, 2021.)

That said, millions of people around the country and the world rejoiced, literally dancing in the streets at the news of Trump's defeat.

Lewd-icrous Rudy

November 25, 2020

For Russia, he served as a gullible tool,
Then Borat confirmed that he's easy to fool.
He thought a young actress was being a flirt—
That's why he endeavored to "tuck in his shirt."

Later he looked like a sinister clown,
Dripping with sweat in a dark shade of brown.

Though sweat that's brunet may be hard to explain,
It's better than lying and having to feign
That the briefing in Philly was meant to take place
At a dingy, deplorable, ludicrous space
That unwittingly bordered an "adult" emporium
And a suitably out-of-the-way crematorium.

His fee for all this, twenty thousand a day,
An amount Trump's campaign is unlikely to pay,
Confirms that he's arrogant, clueless, and vain—
"America's mayor" is full-bore insane.

When he finished as mayor he should have retired—
His "sell by this date" tag has long since expired.

~~~~~~~~~~~~~~~~~~~~~~~~~~~~

The period between the middle of October and the middle of November was a bad interval for Rudy Giuliani, Trump's personal lawyer at the time. First, less than two weeks before the presidential election, Sacha Baron Cohen's sequel to his Borat movie, *Borat Subsequent Moviefilm*, was released. It includes a scene in which Giuliani, after a fawning interview by a young female "reporter," joins her in a hotel room. Presumably believing they are about to become intimate, he lies down on a bed, pulls out his shirt, and sticks his hand down his pants—at which point Borat (Baron Cohen) races into the room and interrupts him. The scene and the uproar it triggered were embarrassing to the man once called "America's Mayor" for his crisis management in the aftermath of 9/11. Giuliani offered a specious explanation: "I was tucking in my shirt."

CUT TO November 7, four days after the election: Giuliani was one of the leaders of the fraudulent "inquiry" into the legitimacy of the election count. Expressing concern over the integrity of the results in Pennsylvania, he called for a press conference at the "Four Seasons" in Philadelphia. Unfortunately (for him—almost everybody else found it hilarious), Trump campaign staffers had specified a small company on the outskirts of Philadelphia called Four Seasons Landscaping, located near a porn shop and a crematorium. There, with a straight face and a real lectern in front of Four Seasons Landscaping's garage, Giuliani read statements and took questions. This venue was not, even slightly, on par with the high-end Four Seasons Hotel in the heart of the city, which was, in all likelihood, the intended location of the event. The Trump team, however, maintained that the landscaping business was the intended venue.

Then, on November 19, at a press conference in which Giuliani (dishonestly) claimed to have evidence of massive voter fraud, his hair product—perhaps a cheap, temporary cover-up or even mascara—liquified and trickled down his face in dark brown streaks impossible to miss.

Giuliani was charging the Trump campaign $20,000 a day to oversee the unfounded election-fraud lawsuits. Later we learned that Trump wouldn't pay the legal fees; he would reimburse Giuliani only for expenses.

Nine Months Into the Pandemic: Coping and Hoping

December 1, 2020

I eat out of doors when it's 40 degrees.
I bypassed Thanksgiving for fear of disease.

I've almost forgotten the basics of grooming.
I do it now mostly for FaceTime and Zooming.

I still go for days without washing my hair;
I look in the mirror and get quite a scare.

My trips to the market are no longer fraught,
And cleaning supplies are now easily bought.

I no longer wipe all my doorknobs and faucets
A dozen times daily to be extra cautious.

I now keep my masks with my bras in my drawers.
(I wear both in public but *not* home indoors.)

I stay in my house countless days at a time.
My sink's full of yesterday's dishes and grime.
In theory I've plenty of time to be clean,
But why should I bother; my mess isn't seen.

There's news of the virus each day on my screens.
It's grim, but there's progress on Covid vaccines.
They've given us promise, a new way to cope,
And also a crucial infusion of hope.

~~~~~~~~~~~~~~~~~~~~~~~~~~~~~~~

Taking stock of the pandemic about nine months into it, we had some answers but even more questions. There were no longer shortages of toilet paper, disinfectants, and cleaning supplies. Our appreciation for grocery-store workers, hospital employees, and other essential workers continued. But what was safe? At the outset, we had worried about transmission of the virus from surfaces, but it turned out that wasn't likely. Was it safe to eat in restaurants? Yes, but only outside. So we did, in cold weather, with masks, jackets, and heat lamps. Most offices, schools, and entertainment venues remained closed, so we stayed home—which meant that personal hygiene, and dressing in a way fit to be seen, suffered. Meanwhile, hospitals remained full and deaths continued. But medical science reported significant progress in the development of a Covid-19 vaccine.

Election Aftershock

December 4, 2020

Frivolous lawsuits and false claims of fraud,
Each of them ludicrous, stupid, and flawed—
Trump's a demented, deluded accuser,
Deep in denial that he is a loser.

Recently pardoned with nothing to do,
Shameless Mike Flynn is proposing a coup—
Martial law first, then a redone election.
Flynn is still eager for Donald's affection.

Even Bill Barr said that Trump was defeated,
Trump, though, maintains that he won and was cheated.
His cultists believe every falsehood he spews,
Relying on lies masquerading as news.

And meanwhile, Biden is forming a crew
Of experts and others who know what to do.
No daughter or son or political hack
Will keep us from getting our decency back.

Did Trump truly believe he won the election, or was his "Stop the Steal" fight a charade designed to convince his followers to remain loyal for a possible 2024 run and other endeavors? Or maybe "Stop the Steal" was a diversion for him, a big mind game to assuage his wounded ego, since "loser" is probably his least favorite word.

Trump and his allies lost more than sixty lawsuits (about fifty as of the date of this poem) alleging election fraud and improper voting processes in multiple states. Judges and legal experts called the lawsuits "frivolous" or "meritless." Even judges appointed by Republicans and by Trump himself rejected the claims.

Michael Flynn, who had been Trump's national security advisor for less than twenty-five days, was in legal trouble for allegedly lying to the F.B.I. about his interactions with the Russian ambassador to the U.S. A few weeks after the 2020 presidential election, while Flynn's case was still pending, Trump pardoned him. A week later, Flynn forwarded a tweet suggesting that Trump declare martial law, suspend the Constitution, and hold a new election under military authority—an outlandish proposal.

Joe Biden, meanwhile, was assembling a staff of advisors who were experienced and knowledgeable, unlike many in Trump's advisory circle, including his daughter Ivanka and her husband.

Vicious and Seditious: "Who, ME?"

December 12, 2020

"That Texas suit was very strong!
Those justices, they got it wrong!
I'm VERY angry at my court!
That suit is NOT my last resort!
I'll fight until I PROVE I won—
You're WRONG if you presume I'm done.
My second term will start up soon,
My lawyer Rudy, no buffoon,
Has found new PROOF to BASE it ON!
(He'll show you when his Covid's gone.)
Yes, FOUR more years of me me me,
It's in the cards, decisively!
But just in case Joe Biden won
I'll use my lame-duck time for FUN:
Arctic drilling! Felon killing!
Filling jobs that don't need filling
With loyal guys, as quid pro quo,
To SABOTAGE and HINDER Joe!
Oh, *I'LL* show JOE who's REALLY boss
As payback for my 'fake news' loss!"

~~~~~~~~~~~~~~~~~~~~~~~~~~~~~~~~~~~

On December 9, 2020, Donald Trump threw his support behind a lawsuit filed by the Texas attorney general asking the U.S. Supreme Court to overturn the electoral results in *other* states—namely, Georgia, Pennsylvania, Michigan, and Wisconsin, all of which Biden won. States can bring lawsuits against others states directly to the U.S. Supreme Court, but the issues in these cases usually concern water rights, border disputes, and other property matters. The Texas attorney general's lawsuit was widely regarded as desperate, baseless, and absurd. The Supreme Court rejected it. Trump seemed to think that the Court, after he had chosen a third of its members, would do his bidding.

Undeterred, Trump's attorney Rudy Giuliani resumed his challenge to the election results, once he was released from the hospital for Covid-19. He claimed to have extensive evidence of election treachery, but his efforts continued to bear no fruit. Meanwhile, Trump undertook actions that seemed intended to spite Biden. For example, after Biden's victory, Trump ordered the execution of several federal prisoners, the last one occurring just days before Biden's inauguration. (Biden has said he will work to end the death penalty.) Trump broke a 130-year tradition of pausing executions during a presidential transition period. In addition, in December, Trump's administration announced that it would auction off drilling rights in the Arctic National Wildlife Refuge in early January. (Biden, on his first day in office, issued an executive order halting the drilling, at least temporarily.) Trump also shoved loyalists into federal posts mere weeks before Biden's inauguration. For example, he appointed former Trump campaign officials to a Pentagon board, after tossing others off. The idea, it seemed, was to hamper government agencies and undermine the upcoming administration. (Trump often capitalizes words randomly, and this poem, in his voice, follows suit.)

Blackwater Pardon Application
(Based on "Chattanooga Choo Choo," starting with the "pardon me" stanza)

December 26, 2020

"Pardon me, Trump,
Though I'm an unrepentant felon,
Guilty of crime,
But I don't wanna do time.

Can you discuss with us
A brazen, baseless pardon?
I shot a crowd
And at the time I was proud.

I'll leave this *God*-forsaken prison with no guilt in my chest.
You *don't* believe in war crimes; that is *why* you're the *best*!
Sorry, dead Iraqis,
We're Erik Prince's lackeys.
Trump, we want our normal-life existence *back*, please."

Other White House Pardon Applications
December 26, 2020

Roger Stone
(Trump advisor, political trickster, and dapper dresser with a huge Nixon tattoo on his back)

"Pardon me, Trump,
'Cause we've been buddies for a long time.
I'll get a tattoo,
No, *not* of Nixon—of you!"

Paul Manafort
*(former Trump campaign chairman who lied to Mueller's investigative
team, perhaps knowing a pardon was in the offing)*

"Pardon me, Trump,
I kept our secrets to myself, man.
Tipoffs to me
Explained how I can be free."

Michael Flynn
*(retired army general who suggested that Trump deploy the military to
"rerun" the 2020 election; Sidney Powell, one of Flynn's attorneys, toiled
deceptively to overturn it)*

"Pardon me, Trump,
And I'll get martial law in action,
Call it a coup.
Watch me and Sidney come through."

~~~~~~

Presidents often grant pardons to people who have (or seem to have) accepted responsibility for their crimes and demonstrated good behavior. Pardons are also used to absolve people who have been of service to a president or are connected to him, regardless of remorse. Most of Trump's late-term pardons were of the second variety.

Trump's Blackwater-massacre pardons drew strong condemnation. Blackwater USA was a private security firm co-founded by Erik Prince, the brother of Trump's Secretary of Education, Betsy DeVos. Blackwater guards were working in Bagdad, Iraq, in 2007 when they opened fire on civilians in the street, killing seventeen and wounding more than twenty. Seven years later, one of the guards was convicted of murder, and three of manslaughter. On December 23, 2020, Trump granted them pardons, and all four were released from prison.

In November 2019, a federal jury found Roger Stone guilty of lying to Congress about conversations he had with the Trump campaign, among other crimes. Trump pardoned Stone on December 23, 2020, having commuted his sentence earlier.

Paul Manafort breached his plea agreement with Mueller's team by lying and withholding information. In 2019, Manafort was sentenced to more than seven years in prison for a variety of crimes. Trump pardoned him on December 23, 2020, sparing Manafort from serving most of his sentence. Many observers believed that Trump had floated the idea of a pardon to Manafort to reward him for his silence and lies in the Mueller investigation.

For Michael Flynn, see the background information for the poem "Election Aftershock" (December 4, 2020), earlier in this book.

2021

2021 opened with a calamitous event: on January 6, a frenzied, insurrectionary mob invaded the U.S. Capitol building in an attempt to overturn the presidential election results and keep Trump in office. The insurrection failed, and Congress certified Joe Biden as the next president, with Kamala Harris making history as the first woman and the first person of color to become vice president. Trump was impeached again, this time for "incitement of insurrection" against the U.S. government, and acquitted again. The pandemic roared on. In a feat of medical bravura, scientists quickly developed vaccines protecting against Covid-19, but they worked only if you got them. (Some people chose not to, as part of an anti-vaccine backlash.) In what seemed a parody of income inequality, one of the richest men in the U.S. spent billions to be launched into space in a rocket made by one of his companies. On the international front, the twenty-year American involvement in the war in Afghanistan came to an end.

Sedition

January 6, 2021 (afternoon)

The brutal mob that Trump induced,
The rioting that he unloosed,
Are very clearly the result
Of stirring up his blinkered cult
With years of angry, vicious lies—
Which makes this chaos no surprise.
Let's hope it opens people's eyes
And serves to hasten Trump's demise.

Consequences

January 6, 2021 (evening)

He coddled white supremacists
And QAnon polemicists,
But Mitch and Pence, they coddled *him*,
Assenting to his every whim.
At last they thwarted Trump's command,
"Allowing" Biden's win to stand,
But Mitch and Pence were much too late
To thwart the mobs who crashed the gate.
The monster, *whom they helped protect*,
Allowed the hordes to surge, unchecked,
And breach the legislative branch,
A sick and deadly avalanche.

~~~~~~~~~~~~~~~~~~~~~~~~~~~~~~~~~~~~

As few Americans will ever forget, on January 6, 2021—the day a joint session of Congress was called to count the electoral votes, normally a quick formality—Trump held a rally in D.C. in which he and other speakers falsely claimed that the election had been "stolen." At Trump's prompting, many in the audience marched to the U.S. Capitol building after the rally. Then, as Americans watched on television, a mob of Trump supporters, some of them armed, stormed the building. At least two thousand made it inside. They assaulted police officers, smashed into the House chamber, and vandalized offices. Some left feces and urine in the hallways. Five people died during the attack or the next day, and hundreds were injured. Four police officers who confronted the rioters later died by suicide. Lawmakers fled from the rioters and did not return to the House chamber until about 3:30 a.m. Vice President Mike Pence then validated the final electoral tally and upheld the election, as he was legally required to do, in spite of Trump's pressure on him to overturn it. Pence and Senate Majority Leader Mitch McConnell condemned the riot. Even so, both of them, especially Pence, had spent four years supporting and enabling Trump, which made it easier for Trump and a slew of his most ardent followers to assemble a mob and ignite the riot in the Capitol.

What's Next?
January 7, 2021

Thirteen days still give the dolt
Time to galvanize his cult
Or start a war or stealth attack—
HELP, I want my country back!

~~~~~~~~~~~~~~~~~~~~~~~~

After the riotous insurrection on January 6 failed to stop the nonexistent "steal" of the 2020 presidential election, many feared that Trump would try something else. With a mere thirteen days left in his term, several administration officials and lawmakers on both sides of the aisle reviewed ways to curtail him, with some contemplating the Twenty-fifth Amendment. (The Twenty-fifth Amendment to the Constitution allows the vice president to step in for the president if the president has been declared unfit for office by the vice president and a majority of the Cabinet.) General Mark Milley, chairman of the Joint Chiefs of Staff, was concerned that Trump might misuse the military to do something rash—perhaps order a military strike or even launch nuclear weapons—and told senior military officers not to take orders from "anyone," unless he, Milley, was involved.

A Con Man from Queens

January 9, 2021

There once was a con man from Queens
Who liked to cause treasonous scenes.
Said some at the riot,
"We would have kept quiet,
But Trump said the end's worth the means."

Someone posed a Trump limerick challenge, and this was the result.

Leaving

January 21, 2021

New York is looking into you.
Your day of reckoning is due.
And maybe Georgia too will bring a claim.
You're nothing but a crime-boss con,
A lying, racist, vulgar Don,
A man who likes to anger and inflame. . . .

There were many times you broke the law,
So many times we thought "last straw."
And all in all, they confirm you're vile.
Every place you went, you stirred up hate,
Those rioters, they took your bait.
So don't return; we're cleaning up the bile.

And now Deutsch Bank won't lend to you,
Your P.G.A. event is through,
But maybe Vlad will never let you down.
You worshipped and admired him,
The same with North Korea's Kim,
Though *both* knew all along that you're a clown. . . .

So bye, Trump, no tears for you,
After what you put us through.
What a joy and thrill to see you go.
Good riddance, *what* a foul reign.
Don't plan on coming back again—
You *brought* us *far* too *low.*

~~~~~~~~~~~~~~~~~~~~~~~~~~~~~~~~~~~~~

On January 20, 2021, the day of Biden's inauguration, Trump left Washington, D.C., on a plane bound for his adopted home state of Florida. He was one of the few presidents in history not to attend the inauguration of his successor.

After the January 6 riot, Deutsch Bank, one of the few banks that still did business with him, severed ties. (Other banks had long refused to work with Trump because, among other reasons, he didn't repay loans.) Likewise, after the riot, the Professional Golfers' Association (P.G.A.) canceled its contract for a major tournament at one of Trump's clubs. The New York Attorney General's office had already been investigating Trump's business dealings. The state of Georgia was considering a criminal investigation into Trump for his attempts to overturn Georgia's election results, including a phone call to pressure Georgia's secretary of state to "find" enough votes to reverse Biden's victory there. (This poem, loosely based on the song "Leaving on a Jet Plane," by John Denver, was inspired by a friend who sang his own version at a Zoom gathering.)

Second Impeachment Trial and Acquittal of Donald Trump
February 9–13, 2021

On January 13, 2021, the House again voted to impeach Trump, this time for "incitement of insurrection" against the U.S. government for his role in encouraging the January 6 attack on the Capitol. The trial in the Senate began on February 9, 2021, and ended in Trump's acquittal on February 13. Seven Republican senators joined all Democratic and Independent senators in voting to convict Trump, but the result was still ten votes short of the two-thirds majority required for a conviction. As significant as the second impeachment and acquittal were, they (like the first impeachment trial) did not inspire a poem.

Cuomosexual Harassment

March 12, 2021

I'm distressed, I'm in shock!
Were you under a rock?
Did you think that MeToo
Had nothing to do
With powerful *you*?

You regarded your aides
Not as brains, but as babes,
If female and youthful.
Please, Andrew, be truthful!

We presumed you'd go far,
A Pandemic Age star,
With those PowerPoint charts
That bestirred viewers' hearts!

So from great heights you fell:
Adulation to hell.
Your late father would cringe
To observe you unhinged.
Your three daughters, aghast—
What if THEY were harassed?

Should you *stay* now or *go*?
Hell, I really don't know.
But the probe from Tish James
With regard to the claims
Should, for certain, proceed,
With commitment and speed,
And perhaps then we'll see
What your future will be.

Early in the coronavirus pandemic, New York Governor Andrew Cuomo received widespread praise for his leadership and his determination to curtail the virus's spread. People eagerly tuned into his daily press briefings to catch up on the latest statistics and trends, illustrated in clear PowerPoint graphics. Media personalities coined the term "Cuomosexual" to describe viewers who admired him. His popularity didn't last long, though. In December 2020, a former aide accused him of sexually harassing her for years. During the next few months, other women—mostly advisors or aides to Cuomo—came forward with similar accusations. In late February 2021, New York State Attorney General Letitia (Tish) James launched an independent investigation of the governor. (Note: On August 3, 2021, almost five months after this poem, Attorney General James released the results of the investigation, which concluded that Cuomo had sexually harassed multiple women. Cuomo denied the claims, but despite his defiance, he resigned later in August. Many leading Democrats had already urged him to do so.)

Afghanistan: Was There No Plan?

August 20, 2021

The Taliban—a vicious clan—
Prevailed in days, with few delays,
While anguished people clung to planes
To flee its ruthless, lawless chains.

U.S. forces were deficient.
Biden's words were insufficient.

Even Milley was surprised.
Was he grossly ill-advised?

Will poppy profits start to fuel
A new regime that's harsh and cruel?

Will women lose their right to work
By atavism gone berserk?
Will men in power overrule
A young girl's right to go to school?

And no one truly can explain
Our twenty years of death in vain.

~~~~~~

The American withdrawal from Afghanistan, after a twenty-year war against the Taliban, was chaotic and deadly. A suicide bomber at the Kabul airport killed thirteen U.S. service members and about 170 Afghan civilians, and an American drone strike accidentally killed ten Afghan civilians. Throngs of Afghans tried to flee the country by pushing their way inside airplanes that were about to depart. Some even clung to the *outside* of at least one U.S. military plane as it took off, falling to their deaths. Even so, more than one hundred and twenty thousand Americans and Afghan allies were safely evacuated.

What surprised everyone—from Biden and Chairman of the Joint Chiefs of Staff Mark Milley on down—was the speed with which the Afghan army fell apart and the Taliban took over the country. American intelligence experts thought that Kabul, the capital, could fall within three months; it took less than ten days. Nonetheless, President Biden defended his decision to pull U.S. troops out of Afghanistan to end the twenty-year war, noting that there would "never be a good time to withdraw U.S. forces." What remained to be seen was whether the Taliban would honor its pledge, made in mid-August, to treat women and girls differently from the brutal, archaic ways for which it was notorious. For example, would the Taliban allow women to work and girls to attend school?

Dan Quayle: Savior of Our Democracy?
(A Tale of Two Veeps from Indiana)
September 17, 2021

Who *cares* if he's awful at spelling!
Back *then* there was nothing foretelling
That Quayle, when he reached his maturity,
Would rise from his longtime obscurity
And warn a V.P. from his state
To soundly reject Donald's bait.

Do we really believe our democracy's fate
Was secured by a guy we considered lightweight?

~~~~~~

Until September 2021, Dan Quayle was mostly remembered for misspelling "potato" when he was George H. W. Bush's vice president. But *Peril*, a book by Bob Woodward and Robert Costa released that month, showed Quayle in a different light. The book revealed that Vice President Mike Pence had asked Quayle, who knew Pence from Indiana political circles, whether there were ways he could comply with Trump's demand to avoid certifying the election results on January 6. Quayle was clear and firm: "Mike, you have no flexibility on this. None. Zero. Forget it. Put it away." And Pence did. Perhaps additional confidants whom Pence consulted gave him the same advice, but since Quayle, in all likelihood, was a source for Woodward and Costa, Quayle got the favorable billing. Pence, of course, had been under intense pressure from Trump, who even tweeted, *while the January 6 riot was underway and lives were in danger*, that Pence lacked the courage to do "what should have been done." As Woodward and Costa wrote, Pence ultimately realized that "acting to overturn the election would be antithetical to his traditional view of conservatism."

This poem also has a limerick version:

Who cares if he's rotten at spelling!
Back then there was nothing foretelling
That V.P. Mike Pence
Would be on the fence
Till guidance from Quayle was compelling!

Facebook (the Other Virus)
October 27, 2021

Reckless brute and global menace
   Tentacles in every crevice
      Reaching, surging, much too far
         Causing strife in Myanmar
            Trouble in the Philippines
               Mental harm to U.S. teens
                  Fueling Trump before the ban
                     Stirring hate in South Sudan
                        Domination, that's the plan
                           Spreading when and where it can
                              No regard to lies and strife
                                 No regard to death and life
                                    Zuck ignores the harm he sows
                                       Long as Facebook grows and grows

~~~~~~~~~~~~~~~~~~~~~~~~~~~~~~~~~~~

Facebook, which in some countries is the main (or only) source of information for the general public, has in recent years been accused of facilitating the spread of disinformation, exacerbating factional tensions, and inciting violence. In Myanmar, for example, Facebook's algorithms promoted posts encouraging violence against political protesters—even after Facebook admitted in 2018 that hate speech and falsehoods on its platform led to violence against Myanmar's Rohingya minority. In the Philippines, the Duterte dictatorship for years used Facebook to spread lies, smear opponents, and discredit critics. In the U.S., Instagram—owned by Facebook—is widely blamed for a significant increase in suicide, depression, and self-harm among teenage girls. Facebook banned Trump after the deadly insurrection on January 6, 2020, but before then, Trump repeatedly used the platform to spread falsehoods and divisive rhetoric.

Facebook founder Mark Zuckerberg acknowledged these trends and pledged to address them. But his commitment to righting wrongs has so far come in second to his commitment to expanding Facebook's power, reach, and profits. (This poem was written right before Zuckerberg changed the parent company's name from Facebook to Meta.)

Gaetz, Gosar, and Greene on the Rittenhouse Verdict

November 19, 2021

"A teenage boy, a deadly gun—
Yep, vigilantes get things done!

Yo, lefty marchers, watch your backs!
This verdict grants us more attacks!

A biased judge, you snowflakes claim?
Well, watch your ass, we've got good aim!

Those guns for war, please give us more!
They'll do the trick when protests soar.

We LOVE the verdict in this trial—
Hooray for patriotic Kyle!"

~~~~~~~~~~

On August 25, Kyle Rittenhouse, a 17-year-old from Illinois, drove to Kenosha, Wisconsin, where a crowd was protesting the shooting of a Black man by a white police officer (non-fatal, this time). Rittenhouse, who is white, carried a semi-automatic, AR-15-style rifle and claimed that he had arrived to protect people and property. An unarmed man chased Rittenhouse into a parking lot, and Rittenhouse shot him four times and killed him. A crowd then pursued Rittenhouse, including a man who attacked Rittenhouse with a skateboard. Rittenhouse shot and killed him also. Rittenhouse then shot and wounded another man.

Some observers believed that the judge in Rittenhouse's murder trial was biased in favor of the defendant. For example, at one point the judge loudly rebuked the lead prosecutor. In any event, the jury, on November 19, 2021, found Rittenhouse not guilty on all charges, and he immediately became a right-wing hero. U.S. Representatives Matt Gaetz (R-FL), Paul Gosar (R-AZ), and Marjorie Taylor Greene (R-GA), three of the House's most ardent far-right agitators, lauded Rittenhouse as a hero. The spectacle of a teenager brandishing a military-style weapon on the street—and killing people with it—seemed not to faze members of a political party once known for respecting "law and order."

Winter in the Time of Covid
(Based on a Recurring True Story)

December 11, 2021

Glasses and earrings and earbuds and mask—
Wearing all four is a difficult task.

My lenses are foggy, a mask strap's undone,
And darn it, my day has just barely begun.

Because it's now winter, I add in a hat.
An earring pops off and it's lost, just like that.

I switch to my earmuffs and find they are worse.
Adjusting their placement, I knock down my purse.

My lipsticks and credit cards scatter around.
I bend to retrieve them and fall to the ground.

My earbuds drop off and they bounce on the floor.
I grab them but find that my arm is still sore—

The pain from the booster is lasting too long
(But worth it to make my immunity strong).

I pick myself up, now with glasses askew.
I straighten their fit, but they fog up anew.

There is *way* too much stuff on my head, face, and ears,
But I'm warm and protected from Omicron fears.

Reports of a new, more transmissible variant of Covid-19—Omicron—prompted renewed caution and more consistent mask-wearing. It also led to more grouchiness because it's hard to wear a mask in winter, with earmuffs and hats on top of earbuds and earrings, not to mention foggy lenses. Nevertheless, grumpy—and even clumsy—mask-wearers understood the importance of protecting themselves and others.

2022

2022 was a turbulent and momentous year. Stunning the world, Russia invaded Ukraine with airstrikes and ground attacks on February 24. Ukrainian President Volodymyr Zelensky galvanized his country to fight back, becoming an international symbol of leadership and courage. In the United States, mass shootings in Buffalo, New York; Uvalde, Texas; and elsewhere rocked the country and rekindled debates about gun-safety measures. There was also good news: in April, the Senate confirmed the nomination of the first African American woman to the U.S. Supreme Court, a triumph marred only by the absurd Republican questions at her Senate confirmation hearings. The Supreme Court was in the headlines again in early May, when someone leaked a draft opinion overturning *Roe v. Wade*, astonishing the country. The Supreme Court's final opinion, issued on June 24, was virtually unchanged from the draft. In the summer and fall, the House committee investigating the insurrection at the Capitol aired public hearings, some with startling revelations about Trump's behavior on January 6, 2021. In August, the F.B.I. executed a search warrant at Trump's Florida home and seized thousands of documents, many marked "classified." In late October, Elon Musk acquired Twitter for $44 billion. Not all outsize headlines involved history-bending or political news: Olympic figure skating faced a doping scandal, and an infamous slap marred the Academy Awards presentation.

Olympic Figure Skating: It Was Ladies' Night and the Feeling's Not Right

February 19, 2022

"WE demand GOLD, we don't CARE how it's done!
'WIN at all costs' is not MEANT to be fun!"
For Putin and Russia, is *that* how it went
At skating's quadrennial prestige event?

Not doing a quad jump is not a debacle.
The same for a fall or a spin with a wobble.
These skaters are human; their art is a sport.
Don't train them to death, and please give them support.
Don't yell at a teen who collapsed under stress,
And a word of advice, NBC and all press:
You did *not* need to show the whole *globe* all that crying.
You may say "public interest"; I say "needless prying."
It is fine to probe training that might be abusive,
But your footage backstage became *far* too intrusive.
Regarding the doping—I hope they unmask
The truth of the matter, a difficult task,
But also, they *need* a corrective approach:
So *please* raise the age, limit quads, can the coach.

~~~~~~

At the 2022 Winter Olympics, one of the headliners was Kamila Valieva, a fifteen-year-old Russian figure skater who combined balletic grace with impeccable quadruple jumps. Heavily favored to win gold in the women's individual competition, she became the center of a doping scandal soon after she helped the Russians achieve gold in the team event. A sample she submitted for a drug test in December tested positive for a medication banned for increasing endurance. (The result came to light during the Olympics.) She was nonetheless allowed to compete in the singles event. The scrutiny and pressure after the drug-test revelation clearly affected her performances. Her short program was flawed, but she still came in first. The long program, however, was devasting for her: she stumbled several times and even fell, finishing fourth overall. When she left the ice in tears, her coach berated her instead of offering support, shocking viewers and even the head of the International Olympic Committee, who hinted that her coaches may have been responsible for the positive drug test. Backstage after the competition, NBC filmed every agonizing minute, broadcasting Valieva's meltdown and exploiting the drama and anguish. Valieva trained with a well-known coach at a strict Moscow skating club known for producing top-tier teenage skaters who can perform multiple quadruple jumps but burn out and retire, with injuries, before age 18. Critics say the Moscow club encourages excessive weight loss and dehydration, among other harsh practices. After the doping scandal, there were calls for reforms in skating, including raising the age for Olympic eligibility and deemphasizing quadruple jumps (for women). Some figure skating commentators also called for punishing or banning the coaches responsible for Valieva's ordeal.

Ukraine

February 27, 2022

Mr. Putin:

You don't invade a country on the pretense that "it's mine."
Is this the 18th century or 1939?
Both *then* and *now* that conduct is *completely out of line*.
But brutal, bold expansion is a part of your design.
Who's next? The Czech Republic? Finland? Maybe Liechtenstein?
What other countries' borders do you want to realign?

You've angered foreign leaders, from the left and from the right.
They're all appalled and shaken by your brazen, senseless fight,
Except for one named Donald Trump, who praised you from the start,
And after your invasion, he rashly claimed you're "smart."

He's jealous of your power, that you're not constrained by rules.
He wishes *he* had no constraints—as did his cult of fools—
When he pressured Pence to break the law and blithely overthrow
The sound and fair election of our former V.P. Joe.
The guardrails of our country worked—but oh, just barely so.

Mr. Trump:

A lot of us believe it's *well* past time for you to go.
You lost a fair election (but pretend it wasn't so).
Play golf and eat your junk food, but it's time to leave the fray.
Our country will be better off if you just fade away.
We're fortunate that Biden is the one now at the helm.
The tragedy in Ukraine would have left you overwhelmed.
And Joe believes in NATO, which you never seemed to get,
Because your buddy Putin thinks that NATO is a threat.
If that's your viewpoint, turn off Fox and watch a balanced show,
Or read a book (for once) and learn that Putin is our foe.
The allies you antagonized are all on Ukraine's side,
And Zelenksy is a hero; did you think he'd flee and hide?

You held up aid to Ukraine in your slimy, vain request,
But Ukraine is much braver than you ever could have guessed.

On February 24, 2022, Russia invaded Ukraine, unleashing missile strikes and heavy ground assaults. Russian President Vladimir Putin claimed that Ukraine did not have the right to be an independent nation. The invasion drew condemnation from leaders across the globe. As president, Trump had antagonized traditional U.S. allies and disparaged NATO, even musing about withdrawing from it. (NATO, the military alliance of the United States, many European countries, and Canada, dates from 1949.) Putin views NATO as a threat and would like to see it weakened. After the invasion, Trump called Putin "smart" and said Russia's strategy in Ukraine was "genius" and "very savvy." After pushback and demands for clarification, Trump called the invasion of Ukraine "an outrage and an atrocity," but placed the blame on Biden for supposedly displaying weakness and on the "not so smart" NATO nations, who "allowed" Putin to get away with the invasion. Trump claimed that the invasion would not have happened if he were still president, because he and Putin get along. Foreign-policy experts disagreed, maintaining that Putin was emboldened after seeing Trump weaken America's relationships with other democracies. They were relieved that Biden—with his foreign-affairs knowledge and respect for NATO—was the leader of the U.S. The strongest show of leadership, however, was from Ukraine President Volodymyr Zelensky, who mobilized his country to counter Russia's invasion. Elements of the military package that Trump threatened to withhold from Ukraine—unless Zelensky investigated the Bidens— were critical to Ukraine's defense against Russia.

Supreme Jerk

March 23, 2022

Ketanji Brown Jackson, in law school with Cruz,
Excelled, as did he, but they held different views.
Ted's tone at her hearing was boorish and zealous,
And *that* is because he is angry and jealous:
He wishes that HE could advance to the Court
'Cause he's *white*, always *right*, and a man of import,
And campaigning for office is grinding and grim,
And his margin of victory last time was slim.
He thinks running for Senate entails too much work—
He'd prefer lifelong *tenure* at being a jerk.

~~~~~~~~~~~~~~~~~~~~~~~~~~~~~

Senator Ted Cruz's questions for Ketanji Brown Jackson at her Supreme Court confirmation hearings were caustic and absurd. He seemed more interested in creating soundbites for Fox News than in asking serious questions. Cruz and Jackson knew each other at Harvard Law School; they were a year apart but overlapped in their service on the school's prestigious law review. Perhaps underlying Cruz's inane questioning was his jealousy of Jackson's supreme achievement. He didn't cruise to victory in his last election; Democrat Beto O'Rourke made a strong showing against him in 2018, in the closest U.S. Senate race in Texas since 1978.

Alopecia at the Oscars

March 28, 2022

The audience was shocked
By what we saw on air:
A stupid joke by Chris
On Jada's loss of hair,
Avenged by husband Will,
Who let his temper flare.

Yes, Chris likes edgy jokes,
But this was dumb at best.
It would have been ignored
With barely any press
If Will had kept his cool
And hadn't dashed onstage
To wallop Chris on air
And show the globe his rage.

Will could have met with Chris
Another day and time,
And told him, "Hey, your joke
Was clearly out of line.
My wife has alopecia,
And that is a disease,
And making fun of illness
Is hateful. Stop it. Please."

～～～～～～～～～～～～～

At the Academy Awards on March 27, 2022, movie star Will Smith walked up to the stage and slapped comedian Chris Rock, who was presenting an award, after Rock made a joke about Smith's wife, Jada Pinkett Smith, and her loss of hair from alopecia. The public soon learned more about alopecia, a disease in which the immune system attacks hair follicles. (Note: I've known about the illness since I was a child because my father had alopecia universalis.)

Fun and Games

April 9, 2022

I *adore* playing Wordle each day.
It can help make the stress go away.
The *world* is a mess
But Wordle's the best—
Though its dopamine hit doesn't stay.

Oh, I wish that that quick high would *last*
And the game weren't over so fast,
So when Wordle is done
And I crave further fun,
I find Spelling Bee's challenge a blast!

From my ongoing Spelling Bee fix,
I've absorbed little insights and tricks.
Is there *anything* better
Than reusing a letter?!
And that's how a word geek gets kicks.

~~~~~~~~~~~~~~~~~~~~~~~~~~~~~~~~

The word game Wordle took the online world by storm in January 2022. On November 1, 2021, there were ninety daily players; by the outset of January, three hundred thousand; and by the end of January, millions. Part of its appeal is that it can be played only once a day. A software engineer developed the game for his girlfriend, never envisioning that it would go viral. On January 31, 2022, the *New York Times* bought Wordle for an undisclosed price in the low seven figures. Wordle gives the successful player a quick high, a fleeting sense of accomplishment. Another once-a-day *New York Times* word game, Spelling Bee, lasts longer and arguably provides greater fulfillment. Unlike most word-scramble games, Spelling Bee allows the player to use the same letter multiple times, which adds to the enjoyment and the challenge.

Supremely Unusual: A Leaked Draft Undoing Roe v. Wade

A Note to the Ladies of America
*From Samuel Alito, Esteemed Member of the Judicial Branch
of the Republican Party*

May 3, 2022

"Ladies, I don't give a sh*t
Privacy will take a hit!
NEXT time I will retrofit
Griswold to my pious views!
You, dear gals, could even lose
MORE than just your right to choose!
WE don't like it when you use
PILLS to minimize "mistakes."
It's WAY past time to put the brakes
On libertines and lefty flakes!"

"Murderesses, Abortionists, and This Is Just Like Plessy"

May 6, 2022

Alito is antediluvian.
He uses olde words that now *prove* he can
Select from old tracts
And pick and choose facts,
Combining them—gracelessly—
To justify—baselessly—
A radical, activist vision
Undoing a major decision,
Reversing a precedent fifty years old
With partisan bias unleashed, uncontrolled.

Sam Alito's Daft Draft

May 10, 2022

He cited a jurist named Hale,
A 17th century male,
Who ordered the death of two "witches."
We wonder why Sam chose to hitch his
Opinion on outdated sources
And smugly and haughtily force his
Beliefs on our wide-ranging nation.
He must enjoy polarization.

～～～～～～～～～～～～～～～

On the evening of May 2, 2022, the news organization *Politico* stunned the nation when it published a leaked, ninety-eight-page draft opinion by Justice Samuel Alito that overturned *Roe v. Wade.* The draft, written in February, contained language that could be construed to question other rights, such as same-sex marriage and the freedom to use birth control,* even though Alito claimed the opinion did not "cast doubt on precedents that do not concern abortion." The draft opinion, caustic and disdainful, was full of cherry-picked and distant history. Alito cited, with favor, Sir Matthew Hale, a seventeenth-century English jurist born around the same time the Jamestown colony was founded (and about a dozen years after Pocahontas). Lauded as a legal scholar but also known as a misogynist, Hale sentenced two women to death as "witches." In addition, Alito favorably mentioned eighteenth-century language that described a woman who had an abortion as a "murderess" ("Gentleman's Magazine," August 1732). In several passages, he used the old-fashioned word "abortionist," with its hints of secrecy and illegality, as if the medical procedure had not been lawful for fifty years. Alito angered many Americans when he explained why *stare decisis*—respect for precedent—did not apply to *Roe*: he maintained that *Roe* is similar to *Plessy v. Ferguson* (1896)—the notorious Supreme Court case that upheld racial segregation—in that both were "egregiously wrong from the start."

Griswold v. Connecticut, a landmark U.S. Supreme Court decision from 1965, ruled that the Constitution protects the liberty of married couples to use contraceptives without government restriction.

The Blood-Spangled Banner
May 31, 2022

A Texan at eighteen can't get
A can of beer or cigarette.
He has to wait till twenty-one,
But eighteen's fine to buy a gun,
A gun designed to kill a crowd. . . .
The N.R.A. has Congress cowed!
It spews its views with poisoned breath
While little kids are shot to death.
These tragic acts of wrath and hate
Are likely to proliferate
When men can saunter through a store
And buy a gun conceived for war,
When lies the N.R.A. has spread
Speak louder than Uvalde's dead,
When N.R.A. donations grow
And trump the pain of Buffalo.

Assault guns, banned in '94,
Are not illegal anymore.
The "right to bear" was misconstrued;
The prudent ban was not renewed.
A gun not meant for sport or play,
A GUN DESIGNED FOR HUMAN PREY,
A gun envisioned to destroy,
Is sold as if it were a toy.
The G.O.P. should be ashamed
That gun-rights zealots have them tamed.
A silent moment's not enough
When laws are needed, sane and tough.

On May 14, 2022, an eighteen-year-old white supremacist shot and killed ten Black people at a supermarket in Buffalo, New York. Just ten days later, in Uvalde, Texas, another eighteen-year-old killed nineteen children and two teachers at an elementary school. Both shooters used semi-automatic rifles similar to military weapons. The Uvalde gunman legally bought his a week before the shooting, the day after he turned eighteen. He purchased a second rifle a few days later. He also had a device that decreased the time required for the trigger to reset. In an essay on June 2, 2022, *Washington Post* columnist Petula Dvorak pointed out that members of the military are required to undergo rigorous training and follow strict protocols to learn how to use assault weapons properly. They have to "empty their weapons and turn them into the armory every night before going to bed." She added that veterans "know that what America is doing right now—letting civilians with zero training buy the same weapons of war—is insanity." Ironically, in August 2019, Texas increased the legal age to buy tobacco products, including cigarettes and e-cigarettes, from 18 to 21. The drinking age in Texas is 21. An underage person caught purchasing or attempting to purchase alcohol can incur steep fines and even jail time.

What about the Second Amendment? The U.S. Supreme Court didn't rule that the Second Amendment gives Americans an *individual* right to own guns *until June 2008*. Many people are surprised to learn that for the first 220 years of our Constitution, there *wasn't* a judicially recognized Second Amendment right to individual gun ownership. As a friend phrased it, that right is newer than the iPhone (which was launched on January 9, 2007). Four justices dissented in the case that bestowed the individual right to gun ownership—*District of Columbia v. Heller* (June 26, 2008). They argued that the majority opinion was "a strained and unpersuasive reading" of the Second Amendment. Yet even *Heller* stated that, "[l]ike most rights, the right secured by the Second Amendment is not unlimited. . . . It is not a right to keep and carry any weapon whatsoever in any manner whatsoever and for whatever purpose. . . . [N]othing in our opinion should be taken to cast doubt on laws imposing conditions and qualifications on the commercial sale of arms." (Note: This poem is an update of one composed on June 13, 2016, in response to the Orlando nightclub shooting.)

Hutchinson's Testimony: Disquieting on Rioting
June 28, 2022

When matters went against his wishes,
The "president" threw food and dishes.
He tried to grab the driver's wheel
To stop the nonexistent steal.

He cared about himself alone
When risks of others' deaths were known:
"Oh, *let* them enter, armed and free—
'Cause they're not coming after ME!"

The 6th attack was well planned out,
And Trump was on their side throughout:
"The rioters did nothing wrong!
The problem is that Mike's not strong!"

The White House counsel, hair on fire,
Was well aware the plight was dire,
But Meadows took a passive stance,
And sought a pardon in advance.

Ms. Hutchinson was sharp and keen,
Perhaps the country's new John Dean.

"It was un-American. We were watching the Capitol building get defaced over a lie."
—Cassidy Hutchinson, June 28, 2022

The public hearings of the House's January 6 committee were arguably the most compelling TV series of the summer of 2022. The sixth public hearing, on June 28, featured a surprise witness, Cassidy Hutchinson, who was a top aide to Mark Meadows, Trump's last White House chief of staff. Her revelations were astounding. She indicated that the January 6 march on the Capitol was planned ahead of time and that Trump's inner circle knew violence was possible. On January 6 itself, Trump was aware that people gathering to attend his rally were armed with AR-15s and other weapons, but he nonetheless asked for lax security screening so that a bigger crowd could enter the area. Hutchinson testified that he said something to the effect of "I don't f'ing care that they have weapons. They're not here to hurt me." Hutchinson also recounted that a White House staffer told her that after the rally, Trump wanted the Secret Service to drive him to the Capitol, and when they refused, he tried to grab the steering wheel and lunged at a Secret Service agent. On December 2020, she saw ketchup dripping down the wall of the White House dining room and a shattered plate on the floor. The valet explained that Trump had a throwing fit when he learned that Attorney General William Barr told the Associated Press that Trump's claims of widespread election fraud were baseless. On January 6, when the crowd was shouting for Vice President Pence to be hung, Hutchinson overheard White House Counsel Pat Cipollone tell Meadows that they had to "do something" to stop it. Meadows responded that Trump "thinks Mike deserves it; he doesn't think they're doing anything wrong," according to Hutchinson. (Later it came out that Meadows sought a pardon from Trump in advance.)

Run, Hawley, Run!

(But Not for President)
   July 22, 2022

Josh Hawley believes he is manly and tough.
I thank the committee for calling his bluff.
He's *not* made of steel; he's just made of fluff—
A hypocrite windbag who lacks the right stuff.
He pumped up his fist to encourage the crowd,
But soon after that, the mob had him cowed.
A gutsier man would have reaped what he sowed,
But *just* when the vandals began to explode,
He sprinted to safety, away from his goons,
Leaving his White House ambitions in ruins.

~~~~~~~~~~~~~~~~~~~~~~~~~~~~~~

The House January 6 committee's last televised hearing of the summer, on July 21, focused on Trump's refusal to call off the rioters at the Capitol, with a choice sidebar featuring Senator Josh Hawley (R-MO). Hawley, who claims that the left considers traditional masculinity to be "a danger to society," has called for a "revival of strong and healthy manhood in America," with an emphasis on time-honored "male" virtues like courage and assertiveness. When the mob was marching to the Capitol on January 6, Hawley walked by and famously pumped his fist in the air as a sign of solidarity and encouragement. At the July 21 hearing, the American public saw footage of Hawley *fleeing* the mob inside the Capitol as it was overtaking the building. That mob, in all likelihood, included some of the very same people he was riling up with his fist pump earlier in the day. Social media went wild with jokes and memes about he-man Hawley's chicken-out hypocrisy when push came to shove.

No Words: The January 6 Committee's Summer Hearings

July 23, 2022

Words seldom fail me.
Now they derail me.

I almost ran out of adjectives this week.

But I listened to the hearings
And said "apocalyptic."
It was even worse than I thought.
I'm now "apoplectic."

I almost ran out of nouns, too.

Narcissist • tyrant
Hatemonger • bully
Psychopath • traitor.

I used every word
Till the meanings were blurred.

American English
Wasn't designed for this.

Nor was America.

~~~~~~~~~~~~~~~~~~~~~~~~~~~~~~~

The public hearings of the House January 6 committee were thorough, well-presented, and damning. They featured riveting and revolting revelations about the riot and the reactions of Trump. (See "Hutchinson's Testimony: Disquieting on Rioting," June 28, 2022.) At the final hearing of the summer, the committee presented strong evidence of Trump's dereliction of duty in refusing to halt the violence at the Capitol, even when Congressional Republicans, his daughter Ivanka, and other aides urged him to tell the rioters to leave in peace. For 187 minutes, Trump watched the violence on television, indifferent to the possibility of destruction, injury, and death.

Revelations

How Low Can He Go?
  August 9, 2022

Trump: I want generals like Hitler's, loyal through and through!
Kelly: No, they tried to kill him. So . . . is *that* what we should do?

———

Trump: Why don't you shoot 'em in the legs, every Black Lives Matter marcher!?
Milley: If you insist we *do* that, I'll announce my own departure.

———

Trump: I want a *big* parade with*out* our wounded on display.
Kelly: But wounded vets are heroes—we should *not* hide them away.

———

Trump: I won and if you don't agree, you're traitorous and silly!
Pompeo: We need to stop the crazies and uphold the guardrails, Milley.

A nonstop flow of books about Trump—by journalists and former members of his administration—appeared in 2022, usually with gripping details about the disorder and dysfunction in Trump's White House. In August, the *New Yorker* published an article by journalists Peter Baker and Susan Glasser, "Inside the War Between Trump and His Generals," a preview of their 750-page book, *The Divider: Trump in the White House, 2017-2021*. The revelations in the article were chilling:

- Trump wanted his generals to be "totally loyal"—like Hitler's, he said, not knowing that Hitler's generals tried to kill him, and not believing John Kelly, Trump's then chief of staff, when Kelly explained the historical truth.

- Trump wanted the military—ten thousand troops and the 82nd Airborne—to subdue Black Lives Matter protestors in D.C.'s Lafayette Square. When General Mark Milley, then chairman of the Joint Chiefs of Staff, refused, Trump bellowed, "Can't you just shoot them? Just shoot them in the legs or something?" After that, Milley composed a resignation letter that denounced Trump for politicizing the military and admiring the type of fascism that America had fought against. Milley, however, didn't deliver the letter and decided not to resign, vowing to "fight from the inside" instead.

- When Trump started planning for a big military parade (see "Little Donald's Big Parade," February 11, 2018), he told Kelly that he didn't want wounded veterans to appear in it because it wouldn't "look good for me," a stance he insisted on even after Kelly explained that wounded veterans are American heroes.

- Mike Pompeo, then Trump's secretary of state, did not believe Trump's claims that the election was "stolen," even though, in public, Pompeo refused to acknowledge that Biden had won. After the election, Pompeo met regularly with Milley in an effort to prevent Trump and the "crazies" (Pompeo's word) from going off the rails in their attempts to overturn the election.

Top Secret!

August 10, 2022

An evil ex-president failed at a coup
And had to determine what else he could do.

He thought he'd take documents, secret as hell,
And then say to Putin, "I've got things to sell."
Or maybe the Saudi crown prince would pay cash
To purchase a classified, top-secret stash
Of nuclear data on friends and on foes,
Plus top-secret golf tips that only Trump knows.

The Trumps think the "deep state," the Dems, and Joe Biden
Commanded the Bureau to see what was hiding
At Trump's big estate: A "witch hunt," they thought.
They never did learn, though they must have been taught,
That POTUS does NOT boss the Bureau around.
A despot would do that, but that is unsound,
Unethical, wrong, un-American too—
The same sort of thuggery Trump tried to do.

～～～～～～～～～～～～～

On August 8, 2022, the Federal Bureau of Investigation executed a search warrant at Mar-a-Lago, Donald Trump's residence and private club in Palm Beach, Florida. The next day, Trump's son Eric claimed that President Biden must have approved the action because, as Eric explained, that's how things worked when Trump was president. As social media users pointed out, Eric Trump's comment seemed to be an inadvertent confession that his father attempted to control the Department of Justice (D.O.J.) in inappropriate ways. U.S. presidents, as Eric didn't understand, normally do *not* use the D.O.J. and the Bureau to go after political rivals. Those entities have long operated independently, free of partisan influence. Biden found out about the Mar-a-Lago search from news reports, the same way the American public did. Some of the documents recovered from

Mar-a-Lago were marked "top secret/SCI" (sensitive compartmented information), a subset of the highest level of classification. A few days before the raid, Donald Trump hosted the Saudi-funded LIV Golf tour at his New Jersey club. None of the Trumps objected to that, in spite of the Saudis' dismal human rights record.

Mar-a-Lago Musings

September 10, 2022

"We have wine and fine cocktails, the ocean and sand,
And the scoop on the nukes in a key foreign land,
And the very best ketchup and beef bourguignon,
And some folders, now empty, their contents all gone!
We have membership fees that my base can't afford,
And some dirt on Macron just in case you get bored.
But the F.B.I. carted the good stuff away
In a partisan break-in that reeked of foul play.
So we filed for help from my judge Aileen Cannon.
(It's a shame she can't offer assistance to Bannon.)
She agreed to award me my own special master
To delay this whole mess and prevent a disaster.
But those D.O.J. lawyers contested her ruling.
In the meantime, the faith of my base isn't cooling!
And my son-in-law called it a paperwork mix-up,
A benign little overblown clerical slip-up.
And the truth is those papers are ALL owned by ME!
It is dumb that the government doesn't agree.
I can show them to Saudis or blackmail a foe,
And, uh, speaking of Saudis, don't YOU wanna know
Why the Saudis gave Jared two *billion* in dough?!
Does he care that Khashoggi was chopped up in pieces?
No, with *billions* at stake, Jared's sympathy ceases.
But there's NO ONE who's treated more poorly than I!
It's unfair, it's a witch hunt, a hoax, and a lie!"

~~~~~~~~~~~~~~~~~~~~~~~~~~~~~~~~~~~

Revelations about the documents the F.B.I. uncovered at Mar-a-Lago kept making the news. Some of the documents were so sensitive that they would normally be locked up and monitored in a secure location; even top national security officers wouldn't have access to them without special clearance. One recovered document even described a foreign country's nuclear capabilities. The F.B.I. also found four dozen *empty* file folders marked "classified." A curious item on the inventory of recovered documents was labeled "info re: President of France," Emmanuel Macron. (Trump reportedly bragged for years that he had "intelligence" on Macron's sex life.) Trump sued to ask a federal judge to authorize an outside watchdog (known as a "special master") to review the seized documents. The Department of Justice (D.O.J.) opposed the request, but the Trump-appointed judge, Aileen Cannon, sided with Trump. She also blocked the D.O.J. from continuing its review of the materials until the completion of the special master's examination—a delay that could pose security risks. On September 8, the D.O.J. asked the judge to revisit her decision and lift the block. (Ultimately, about two and half months after this poem, an appeals court overturned the appointment of the special master, a loss for Trump.) Also on September 8, not even two months after his conviction for contempt of Congress, former Trump advisor Steve Bannon was indicted in New York for defrauding donors to a "build the wall" organization. Jared Kushner, Trump's son-in-law, downplayed the investigation of the Mar-a-Lago documents as an "issue of paperwork." A few months after Trump left the White House, a fund led by the Saudi crown prince invested two billion dollars in Kushner's new private-equity firm. An advisory panel for the Saudi fund objected to the investment because Kushner was inexperienced, but the Saudi crown prince nonetheless authorized it. The crown prince had built a friendly relationship with Kushner when the latter was a White House advisor, and Kushner stood by the crown prince even after the C.I.A. concluded that the prince had ordered the murder of *Washington Post* journalist Jamal Khashoggi (who was ambushed, killed, and dismembered in October 2018).

Musk's Musings

October 28, 2022

"Look at ME! I bought Twitter! I'll make it my own,
A revised public forum on everyone's phone!
Should I *un*-banish Trump? Maybe Alex Jones too?
That means *hate* speech and falsehoods will flourish anew!
I'm an ardent believer that speech should be free,
But yes, *mostly* when *that* means more *money* for me!
I know TikTok is hotter—but not for much longer.
I will do what it takes to make Twitter grow *stronger*.
And if *that* doesn't happen, however I try it,
I will go after TikTok and venture to buy it.
And if Facebook continues its steady decline,
I will fix it as soon as I make sure it's mine.
But the Bezos be*he*moth is not on my list.
(Have you noticed my rockets are better than his?)
I have eight or nine children with three or four mates.
(I am *much* more attractive than Bezos or Gates.)
Yes, I work night and day, but it's vital to breed
And distribute my premium, genius seed.
I think Microsoft's boring, too dull to acquire,
And while Gates is a nerd, I'm a brash ball of fire.
For now *Twitter's* my baby to nurture and grow,
And the whole globe is watching how far I will go."

~~~~~~~~~~~~~~~~~~~~~~~~~~~~

After a saga that included reneging and a lawsuit, Elon Musk—known for Tesla and SpaceX—became the owner of Twitter on October 27, 2022. Musk calls himself a free speech absolutist. Right-wing Republicans cheered the acquisition, believing that Musk would reinstate Trump and people with similar views who had been banned from the platform. The left feared that Twitter in Musk's hands would poison the country's discourse with hate speech and disinformation. In 2022, TikTok was the ascendant social-media platform, with Facebook struggling and even imitating some of TikTok's well-liked features. Even so, Facebook has many more users in the U.S. than Twitter does. Musk is known for his extreme work ethic; reportedly, he often puts in one hundred hours a week and expects his employees to work at least eighty. His personal life is complicated. For example, he has children with at least three different women. He believes there is an "underpopulation crisis," with too many "good, smart people" not procreating.

Denial: Reflections on the Eve of the Midterm Elections

November 7, 2022

I'm living in a land that's called Denial.
You're welcome to come visit for a while.
The locals speak with eloquence and reason.
The climate is delightful every season.
The air is fresh and clean; the rain is mild.
The waterways are clear and undefiled.
The Lexapro is plentiful and free,
But no one needs it here, not even me.
And people from all backgrounds get along.
They live long lives; their healthcare's very strong.
Elections feature meaningful debate.
There's not a side that whips up fear and hate.
And no one says they've won when they have lost
And tries to get a valid outcome tossed.
Unfounded news is never on TV,
And Twitter trolls and bots have ceased to be.
This paradise is very hard to find. . . .
I wish it were a place outside my mind.

~~~~~~~~~~~~~~~~~~~~~~~~~~~~~~~~

Democrats and moderates were fretful and uneasy before the November 8 midterm elections. Pollsters, pundits, politicians, and the press predicted a red wave—a Republican takeover of Congress and many state offices. Midterm elections usually favor the party that is not in the White House. Adding to the anxiety were Biden's not-so-high approval ratings and voters' concerns about inflation and the economy. In addition, Republicans stoked fear by blaming Democrats for a rise in violent crime. What's more, Republicans who supported Trump's "Big Lie" of a "stolen" election were candidates for positions overseeing and certifying presidential election results in key battleground states—such as Arizona, Michigan, Nevada, and Wisconsin—that Biden narrowly won in 2020.

If these election deniers were to win, they could manipulate the results in the 2024 presidential election in favor of electors representing their preferred candidate. Many people feared that our democracy itself was at stake, and some daydreamed about a different world.

The Red Wave That Wasn't
November 13, 2022

Instead of a red wave, we saw a red puddle.
The drubbing that Trump took was not even subtle.
Civility won, and democracy too,
And just when we thought our republic was through!
Election deniers met well-deserved fates—
They failed to win office in battleground states.
In Nevada, we waited with patience and fear
And wept in relief when the winner was clear.
The Dems kept the Senate in spite of the doubt,
And pundits and pollsters lost credence and clout.

~~~~~~~~~~~~~~~~~~~~

In spite of the predictions and expectations (see the description with the prior poem), the midterm elections on November 8 did *not* result in a red wave. Several Trump-endorsed candidates lost, including nominees for the U.S. Senate in Arizona and Pennsylvania and for governor in Arizona, Michigan, Pennsylvania, and Wisconsin. Leading Republicans blamed Trump for the party's poor showing. In addition, voters in important battleground states rejected election-denying candidates who pushed Trump's "Big Lie" and sought to control their states' electoral systems. (Election deniers did win in less critical states.)

The large number of mail-in votes meant that the results of several key races were not known until after Election Day. On November 9, the vote count for the U.S. Senate race in Georgia resulted in a runoff scheduled for December 6. The races in Arizona and Nevada—and control of the Senate—were still up in the air. After Democrat Mark Kelly won in Arizona on November 11, all eyes turned to Nevada, where a Democratic win would give the Democrats the fifty seats they needed to retain the Senate, regardless of the outcome in Georgia. If, however, the Republican won in Nevada, the Georgia runoff would determine Senate control. No one wanted to wait in panicky suspense until December. The Republican candidate in Nevada was ahead in the count on Election Day, but tens of thousands of ballots from the state's urban areas remained to be tallied. Finally, late in the day on November 12, the Nevada Democratic candidate, Catherine Cortez Masto, won, clinching the Senate for the Democratics. Celebratory texts, emails, calls, and at least one poem (this one) appeared on the phones of liberals and moderates throughout the country. Republicans did capture control of the House from the Democrats, but with one of the smallest swings in years. All in all, Biden had the best midterm results of any president in two decades.

Congressional News Service
(*Sneak Preview of* 2023)

January 25, 2023

Cerebral Adam Schiff's not *up* to *par*,
But loopy Taylor Greene's become a *star*!
She now is BFF with craven Kevin,
Like pigs in s**t or maybe seventh heaven.
She sees the searing threat of Jewish lasers,
While Santos, clad in classic preppy blazers,
Is *not* too low to garner Kevin's blessing. . . .
I find this topsy-turvy mess depressing,
Except that little part about cross-dressing.
But still, my anxious brain needs decompressing,
So time to stay away from news un*less*
More lucid, prudent minds reclaim success.

~~~~~~~~~~~~~~~~~~~~~~~~~~~~~~~~~~~

The opening days of the new, Republican-controlled House were chaotic. Kevin McCarthy (R-CA) failed to win a majority of the votes for Speaker on the first ballot—the first time a Speaker was not elected on the first ballot in a hundred years. He finally became Speaker on the fifteenth ballot, after making concessions to some of his far-right colleagues. Soon, McCarthy kicked Adam Schiff (D-CA) off the House Intelligence Committee. Far-right attention-seeker Marjorie Taylor Greene (R-GA) landed committee assignments, even though she, at times, supported QAnon, 9/11 conspiracy theories, and other false narratives. Her appointment to the Homeland Security Committee seemed preposterous in light of her suggestion that Jewish space lasers caused California wildfires. Yet she and McCarthy had formed a surprisingly close alliance. George Santos (R-NY) was named to committees, even though he had lied about his education, employment history, religion, financial status, check-fraud problems, charitable work, and performance as a drag queen in Brazil. (He withdrew from the committees on January 31, 2023.)

Older

and

Other

Poems

On Hillary Clinton

This poem, written well before Hillary Clinton was a U.S. presidential candidate, secretary of state, or U.S. senator, summarizes Bill Clinton-era indignities and mysteries, without as much sympathy for Hillary as one might expect.

Strife Wife
1998

With a J.D. from Yale
Did she need a strong male
To achieve her ascent
And to co-pay the rent?

When she rode in Bill's wake
Did she make a mistake?
She banked on his power
But soon things turned sour.

With Whitewater woes
And health reform foes,
And hairstyle switching
And Gennifer snitching . . .

Commodity fix-ups
And Filegate mix-ups
And Tyson Food payoffs
And Travelgate layoffs.

Could it *get* any worse,
For the Bill Clinton curse?
Then it did—Paula sued,
And said Bill acted lewd.

But it wasn't pure hell
Until Monica L.

She thought that by kneeling
She'd break the glass ceiling,
Or maybe she'd earn
A plum job from Vern.

Bill claimed it was moral.
(Why not, it's just oral.)
But he parsed every word
Till the meanings were blurred.

They never thought Starr
Would get quite this far
But at length he reported
The mundane and the sordid.

While Bill self-destructed
And Congress erupted
His number-one fan
"Stood by" her man.

She stood by and smiled
While hubby defiled
His office, his life,
His family, his wife.

～～～～～～～～～～～～～～～

Hillary Clinton is an intelligent, dedicated, and accomplished public servant with a chain of achievements that might have led her to become the first female president of the United States. She is also, of course, the wife of Bill Clinton, a savvy politician and not-so-savvy philanderer and dissembler. Some think that Hillary would have gone further faster without Bill, but others believe that, given her ambitions, it was beneficial to marry a man endowed with one of the most brilliant political minds of their generation, his flaws notwithstanding. (For context: In 1969, the year Hillary started law school, only about 7% of entering law students were female. During her law school years, the number of women in the U.S. Senate ranged from zero to two.) Throughout her husband's campaigns and presidency, Hillary struggled to master her tricky balancing act of being a feminist without being "too much" of a feminist, i.e., the kind who might turn off too many voters. In 1992, during Bill's first campaign for president, Hillary claimed that she was "not some little woman standing by her man," as in Tammy Wynette's famous country song, but that's what she did during the Monica Lewinsky matter. Did she do it out of love and devotion, or to preserve an astute political partnership? Perhaps both.

On John McCain and Sarah Palin

After John McCain named Sarah Palin as his running mate, he was just as surprised as everyone else was.

Country Worst
October 11, 2008

Though he pledged country first
He delivered the worst

And the G.O.P. netted
A vixen unvetted—

She's a demagogue ditz
Who gives Democrats fits.

Then with Katie she stumbled
And the right was soon humbled.

She was savvy on shootin'
But so foolish on Putin.

Would the V.P. debate
Serve to seal her fate?

With the bar set so low
Sarah put on a show.

With a wink, she said "Joe,"
To unsettle her foe

But Joe Biden excelled
And the worries were quelled.

Yet her populist shtick
For the right did the trick.

She avoided disgrace
And she stayed in the race.

But her role grew more vicious—
An attack dog malicious.

She would rally the base,
And remind them of race

And then stir up their hate
With her Horton-type bait.

When the Rove-ites uncorked her,
The left should've borked her!

Yet we all thought McCain
Would have utter disdain
For a gutter campaign
That would sputter and wane.

Does he rue his rash bet
On an unknown brunette?

He unleashed a new force
Whom he'd never endorse

But she won't go away
And she'll never obey
The top G.O.P. brass
With her populist sass.

She is basking in fame—
She's quite good at this game.

She was John McCain's tool
But she's nobody's fool.

When John McCain ran for President in 2008, his slogan was "Country First"—a sentiment he presumably believed in. What he (and those advising his campaign) apparently didn't believe in was "thoroughly vet your possible vice-presidential candidate." On the surface, his selection of Alaska Governor Sarah Palin was defensible, if not canny: she was popular in her state, telegenic, female, feisty, and young. Under the surface, though, she started out problematic and got worse from there. Her early media interviews were disastrous, especially those with Katie Couric. Palin fumbled her answers, and was even unable to name the newspapers (if any) that she read. Thus her prospects for the televised debate against Democratic vice-presidential candidate Joe Biden did not augur well. However, to the tremendous relief of Republicans, Palin held her own, delivering an energetic, folksy performance that was on message and free of blunders, though not up to Biden's level in substance. Biden, with experience under his belt, handled Palin's good-ol'-gal posturing with aplomb, and overall he delivered the stronger performance. In the weeks following the debate, Palin amplified her attack-dog role. Ultimately, though, she turned out to be uncontrollable by her G.O.P. campaign handlers—a "rogue" (*Going Rogue* is her political memoir) and a firebrand who drew cheering crowds wherever she went and attracted voluminous media attention. Whether or not McCain deserved better, America certainly did.

On Law School

For anyone who attended law school.

Law-Full
2010

Not knowing much about the law,
We entered law school full of awe.
The first week was a shock and blur
(I know my classmates would concur).
The law, we thought, was serious,
So noble and mysterious,
With cases that would change the land
And men with names like Learned Hand!
Believe me, we were really floored
That law was not "all *Brown v. Board*."
It turned out to be off the wall
With Palsgraf and the fire ball,
And Hawkins and his hairy hand,
And poison trees of contraband.

Penumbras, perpetuities
And other ingenuities,
All tested our acuities
For artful ambiguities.

The law's a seamless web, we learned,
Replete with stones we all unturned.
By *third* year, though, we broke taboo
And left unturned a stone or two,
And landmarks such as *Marbury*
Meant less to us than BAR/BRI.
But still, we aimed to learn (and earn)
And doing well was our concern.

We clerked and worked and knew we should
Encourage justice when we could.
We also learned a legal mind,
Though sometimes skewered, mocked, maligned,
Will serve you well on any journey,
Yes, even as a poet who's
    no longer an attorney.

~~~~~~~~~~~~~~~~~~~~~~

This poem is a flashback for those who attended law school. (Note: Lawyers say "Brown vee Board," not "versus.")

On David Petraeus

Less than a week after the 2012 presidential election, the press fixated on another topic: General David Petraeus, a fine, upstanding public servant until he wasn't.

A Modern Four-Star General
November 13, 2012

From high atop the C.I.A.
And not a secret hideaway,
Transmitting racy emails out,
Petraeus was a fool, no doubt,
To think he'd have the pull and clout
To secretly betray and flout
The C.I.A. and Army rules . . .
But love-struck men are always fools.
As Doctor Freud would surely say,
Petraeus had an urge to stray
And let the country know that he
Is more than what we plainly see:

Commander in Afghanistan,
The author of a "counter" plan.
An expert on insurgency,
So calm in an emergency.
Authoritative in Iraq,
Unruffled by a ground attack.
A modern major general
Whose feats are not ephemeral!

But David wanted even more!
He showed the troops that he could score,
And do it underneath a desk
With someone fit and statuesque!

In prior wars, our men were told,
Be watchful, wary, and controlled,
And don't be charmed by swaying hips
'Cause slips from lips might sink our ships.

Yet David opted to adore
A biographic paramour.
A West Point grad who earned his trust
Became the object of his lust.
Her well-honed brain and well-toned arms
Were chief among her many charms.

The Broadwell broad is army-trained,
So disciplined and well restrained,
Yet envy made her lax and mean,
Behaving like a jealous teen.
Her careless emails were the start
Of how her lover fell apart.
A female email trail derailed
An Alpha male who clearly failed
To live up to his mythic hype–
The noble leader archetype.
Perhaps that image all along
Was propaganda, false and wrong.

～～～～～～～～～～～～～

Known for his expertise in the "counterinsurgency" doctrine, David Petraeus is a
retired four-star Army general who served as commander in Afghanistan and Iraq.
In September 2011, he became the director of the Central Intelligence Agency
(C.I.A.). At some point, he began an extramarital affair with Paula Broadwell, a
West Point graduate, former military officer, and writer working with Petraeus on
his biography. In May 2012, a Tampa woman reported to the F.B.I. that she was
receiving anonymous harassing emails. The F.B.I. discovered that the disturbing
emails were from Broadwell. During the investigation, the F.B.I. also uncovered

evidence of the affair between Petraeus and Broadwell, including an email referencing "sex under a desk." As a result, Petraeus resigned from the C.I.A. in November 2012.

On Poetry and Writing

Can a light-verse poet write a serious poem?

Seriously

Summer 2020

I tried to write a solemn poem
On love and longing, hearth and home,
With similes and metaphors
And words that soar like music scores,
Evoking wistful, mellow moods
Without clichés or platitudes,
With consonance and assonance
And somber sounds of sibilance.
I strove for perfect anapest,
Though scansion's quite a scary quest.
I probed old poems to hone my brain
And open my creative vein.
The fog is cat-like, roads diverge—
I thought my lyric skills would surge!
Yes, hope has feathers, Keats had urns,
But my attempts reaped no returns.
I wrote all night, from dusk to dawn,
Extinguishing each sign and yawn.
The lines I wrote while at my desk
Were grandiose, obtuse, grotesque.
I tried to simplify my style
And sprawled out on my rug awhile.
I thought, while writing on the floor,
Each draft surpassed the one before!
I took a break, reviewed my verse,
And gasped—in truth, each draft was worse!
I tore my drafts up, shred by shred,
And conjured up this poem instead.

W. B. Yeats said, "Out of the quarrel with others we make rhetoric; out of the quarrel with ourselves we make poetry." Thus, this: a pseudo-serious poem about trying to write a serious poem. It comes out against platitudes and clichés while enlisting platitudes and clichés. It makes fun of topics that amateur poets commonly choose, such as "love and longing." It refers to famous poems, such as Emily Dickinson's "Hope is the thing with feathers" and Robert Frost's "The Road Not Taken." It uses (and perhaps overuses) assonance and alliteration. Although the poem refers to the anapest metrical foot (two unstressed syllables followed by a stressed syllable), it employs iambic tetrameter (four metric feet, each containing an unstressed syllable followed by a stressed one). The poem also describes the frustrating process of writing: drafts and more drafts, and the difficulty of judging one's own work. In the end, the poem accounts for nothing except its own existence.

Acknowledgments

I seldom *intend* to write a poem. Instead, a phrase or a couplet materializes in my brain, unbidden, and then I go to work, adding verses, rewriting, and fine-tuning the rhyme and meter. Many people help me along the way. I am grateful to Marie Lefton for her thorough and detailed feedback. I also thank my other "feedbackers"—Amy Fine Collins (my sister), Marilyn Mufson, and Emily Soltanoff—for their wisdom and discernment. I am grateful to my parents, Harold J. Fine and Elsa Honig Fine, for encouraging me and believing in me in many ways. They introduced me to Tom Lehrer and Cole Porter—word wizards and lyricists *par excellence*—when I was a child. Lehrer and Porter undoubtedly had an influence on me; I spent countless hours listening to their vinyl records on the family stereo. My maternal grandfather, Sam Honig, was also an influence. He wrote poetry as a sideline, and his work was published in a local newspaper. I also thank everyone who reads my poems—friends, relatives, neighbors, strangers—and sends comments. I appreciate your encouragement more than you know.

About the Author

Erika S. Fine is a writer and editor. Her poems have been published in Cognoscenti, the "ideas and opinion" site from WBUR, one of Boston's NPR stations; *Light* (a journal of light verse); and the *New York Times*. Her prose has appeared in the *Boston Globe*. She has also been a vintage jewelry dealer, corporate executive, and lawyer. She lives in Brookline, Massachusetts, a short walk from the Boston border.